Reinventing

Myself

A Memoir

Reinventing

Myself

A Memoir

Janet

Goleman

Felgoise

Legacy Books

Contents

Contents

Contents

Why a Memoir?

IN JANUARY 2020, AFTER I'D BEEN DIAGNOSED with cancer at the age of 81, I gathered my four sons to share the news with them. Soon after, I realized that the history I had been creating of my own life, from birth to the present day, which I had been working on in various writing groups, finally had a clear reason for existing.

It wasn't just for me anymore, to reminisce and play with and wrestle to the page; it should become a gift to my sons, perhaps my final way of letting them know who I am, who I have been, and what legacy, if any, I might leave for them and their families to learn from and enjoy. In fact, I'm pretty sure I have at least a few friends and acquaintances who might also be interested in reading this memoir.

That said, I am not so full of myself that I think the world cannot live without me, although at some point it will find out if this is actually possible. In the meantime, I suppose I have lived an unusual life, full of unexpected circumstances, especially for a woman in our society, and that there may be some inspiration somewhere for a young girl to think bigger than she may have otherwise allowed herself to do.

As I was working on all of this, I noticed that it was missing something fundamental. Although I had carefully recounted my development and achievements, I hadn't made any reference to how my life related to these historic events, which occurred concurrently during the years I was reviewing and writing about.

What a great avenue to reflect on my experiences and at the same time share how these world events impacted my life! This approach made the idea of a memoir more meaningful for me and as a former teacher, who could argue with a little education thrown in for my readers?

Within my own sphere, I applauded my unique decision about how to contextualize my memoir. Thankfully, it won't just be about me! I even took it a step further and decided that instead of commencing this whole endeavor with my birth, I would start with the moment that became the single biggest turning point of my life.

"That's it! I got it!"

I knew I was on to something, that this was the best approach, the most revealing way to re-introduce myself to my own family and allow people new to me a window into what inevitably made me who I am today.

But all of the talent, perseverance and strength I found necessary for my survival did not magically appear in the heat of the moment. Those ingredients had been tucked away in my DNA, formulated and passed down from my grandparents to my parents and to me.

Just when I needed them most, my inherited ancestral genetic pool forged its way through my bloodstream, pulsating with all its survival tactics to arm my consciousness with the tools and wherewithal to somehow cope. Through the process of recounting this personal history, I have finally answered the gnawing question of how I was able to survive and surmount my greatest challenge—providing a safe space and survival mechanism for my family!

This inspirational solution provided the answer to my second dilemma: how to re-enter my own story, expand my memoir, and make it relevant and meaningful, which I hope it is for you. Each of us looking to share our stories must delve backward into the historic timeline of our family ancestry and use it to provide context for how we came to be who we are today.

I will begin with this fateful turning point and as I work my way forward in time, I will illustrate how ancestral strength enabled my immediate family to handle our tragedy. I have tried my best to relate the history of my family's brave, courageous actions, which I inherited, and which played a central role in own capacity meet my challenges, one hundred years later!

Eureka!

I found my new pathway to re-enter my memoir and now may I invite you to embark on this journey with me at your side.

Bon voyage!

The Felgoise Family's Date with Infamy

MY SCREAMING WOKE UP OUR FOUR SONS, aged 12 to 16, who rushed from their bedrooms to witness what would soon become our joint nightmare. As my family imploded right there in our bedroom, chaos rained down on our house, punctuated by the pathetic outbursts of emotion and anguish emitted by me and my boys as we witnessed their father's heart attack.

We tried to help him breathe but we had no idea what we were doing.

"Run for Aunt Maureen, across the street," I hollered.

Roy ran barefoot to seek help from our neighbor, a fire company volunteer.

The others clutched my husband's hands while I pounded on his chest.

"Call 911," I screamed, as Brian ran for the phone.

Although the ambulance arrived quickly to whisk him away after initially resuscitating him in the house, Bert Felgoise died that night before he even reached the hospital.

April 27, 1982. He was 46 and I was 44.

I was driven back home from the hospital in a police car, still in shock, but quite aware that I was facing the most frightening time of my life. Apparently, the boys hadn't been able to sleep after the emergency van had departed. I found them sitting together in the den, exactly where I had left them hours before, nervously waiting my return.

The five of us cried uncontrollably, screaming out our pain as I told them the tragic news, that their father had died on the way to the hospital. As the sun came up and the day wore on, tensions escalated and rose higher than those we had experienced during the torturous events of the past 24 hours. We could barely speak of what we had witnessed during those darkened hours.

Our new reality was setting in fast as we stumbled about from room to room, mumbling to each other between my tearful outbursts.

"Why? How could this happen to a man who was only 46?"

No answer.

"What's going to happen to us?"

Nothing.

"Who will run Pine Woods Construction development now?"

No answer.

"Who will take over his law practice?"

Nothing.

We were all so dumbfounded.

The following day flashed by as if we were actors in a silent movie. No one has memories of any dialogue, just flickering images of the Rabbi's visits as well as many neighbors and friends, pouring in and out of our house, nodding, frowning, wiping tears away and mumbling words I will never remember.

We found temporary relief from our misery when the funeral director gave us an assignment to complete that same day. This task forced us to face reality and muster whatever energy we had to come together as a team and select a burial site at Shalom Memorial Cemetery, located near our home in Huntingdon Valley.

Ironically, this cemetery was located directly behind the Pine Woods Housing development, which Bert had been constructing.

We poked our heads above the clouds of doom surrounding us, as we set out in search of the ideal location for burying our beloved Bert Felgoise, husband and father.

"This is it, Mom, Brian said. "It looks right onto Levy Lane, the last street in the development, named for his best friend, our Uncle Bernie."

"How about facing him in a site behind the street with my name?" said Glenn.

"We'd never agree to select an area behind one of the streets that bears our own names," Marc said, as he concluded that conversation before it really got started.

"Yep," I said, "I think Dad would like to look out over Levy Lane."

We ended up selecting a prominent place in the cemetery, directly behind Bert's housing project, where each street bore a different son's name. Finally, here was something to bring out a slight smirk among us, amidst the horror film we were all enduring in real time.

Two days later, on April 29, 1982, I sat in the middle of my two younger boys, with an older brother on each side of them, at the funeral of Bert Melven Felgoise, held at Temple Judea Synagogue on North Broad Street.

We were numb as more than five hundred attendees paraded by to offer sympathy and condolences. The Rabbi and a few dear friends spoke fondly about our beloved and his generous contributions to many organizations.

The Rabbi also read a poem I had created, illuminating Bert's life. The act of writing it had given me a chance to temporarily channel my grief into something productive but hearing it recited only made the reality of Bert's death sink in deeper.

My Poem for Bert

There was a special principal in junior high,
Who inspired Bert, in his life's campaign,
To generously give of himself.
No friend could he deny.
THAT'S HOW WE'LL REMEMBER HIM.

Hard work came easy; he always set a goal.
First a car, then college and Temple Law.
Supporting himself was an act of pride,
Adding to his manhood and leadership role.
THAT'S HOW WE'LL REMEMBER HIM.

REINVENTING MYSELF

Bert's law career and business adventures
Brought opportunity and experience galore,
Jersey Devils, restaurant and meat store,
To provide his loved ones with much more.
THAT'S HOW WE'LL REMEMBER HIM.

Bert's love of four sons recognized no bounds,
Pride, support, and encouragement too,
His parenting set values to last their lifetimes,
Ever present with inaudible sounds.
THAT'S HOW WE'LL REMEMBER HIM.

Creating Pine Woods was a dream come true.
His pride in this community was clear,
Bert rose to the economy's challenge,
For the completion, he hoped to see through.
THAT'S HOW WE'LL REMEMBER HIM.

Bert's reputation increased with involvement:
Republican Party, township, synagogue, too.
As a B'nai B'rith supporter, no call went unheard,
His energy level just didn't relent.
THAT'S HOW WE'LL REMEMBER HIM.

Beloved husband, adoring father,
athletic fan supreme
He followed his boys to field, court and pool.
His support of their games was his number one joy,
There, his working hours were redeemed.
THAT'S HOW WE'LL REMEMBER HIM.

To finish this tribute requires your aid,
For each of us has his/her own story to tell-
Of how Bert Felgoise affected your life.
Keep sharing these tales, so his legacy won't fade.
BECAUSE, THAT'S HOW WE'LL REMEMBER HIM.

––––––––––––––––

The boys and I, along with other family mourners and particularly close friends, were essentially paralyzed by the shock of the funeral, which was the second terrifying experience we had endured in a matter of days.

At the end of the synagogue service, we all realized for the first time that we would never again be a normal family. While driving to the cemetery, we shared how we would handle our farewells during the burial portion of the funeral.

The mourners formed a moving wall, temporarily separating the five of us from the sight of the black coffin, as they trudged by in a line to pay their final respects. We hadn't yet recovered from the trauma of selecting the burial plot and we barely understood the events being played out before us.

Bert's final resting place provided consolation for us all because we intuitively knew he would be pleased with the special site his sons had selected. This belief provided the only inkling of peace to be found that day.

If I could have assigned a soundtrack for that day it would have begun with the lyrics of the song, "Bewitched, Bothered and Bewildered," which best described me as "beguiled again, a whimpering, simpering child again" on that April day in 1982.

The weeks and months that followed were certainly less dramatic than the night Bert died and the trauma that followed, full of screaming and chaotic attempts to revive him, but they were plenty frantic and intense as I had so much to deal with, not only with mourning, but closing many open business wounds as well.

As soon as the seven-day *shiva* period ended, real life demands penetrated the bubble of our distraught lives. First came the fallout from Bert's existing law practice and chasing down the law associate who had absconded with client files. Then I became immersed in business emergencies in reaction to the demands of the mortgage company and harassment from the bank, regarding the fate of a multi-million-dollar construction loan to Bert, who had been the primary developer of the Pine Woods Construction Company. The future of our home, also used in the collateral mix of the construction loan, was yet another worry.

"Was the property to be sold?"

"Could I retrieve client files removed from Bert's office?"

"Would our home, listed as collateral on the loan, be involved in a foreclosure?"

"Would the residential construction business revive, considering the current 1982 mortgage interest rate of 21 percent?"

The questions were relentless.

A rescue team, led by my attorney brother-in-law, financial supporters and others, charged in to tackle the imposing challenges of our family's future. Our close friends, as well as Bert's clients, who owned another construction company, refused our request to purchase and complete Pine Woods development, which would have alleviated our financial conundrum.

To no one's surprise but my own, they turned down our request for help. What a way to learn a practical business lesson: a business deal always trumps friendship. The other company was able to purchase the property at "fire sale" prices instead of paying the real value.

Somehow, during each step I was forced to take, I pretended to create a safe environment for our four teenage boys so they could somehow continue on with their evolving lives.

Looking back on this horrific time of my life, I wonder how I could possibly have coped with all of the demands bombarding me. Having been raised as a pampered, spoiled child, I had no experiential background to prepare me for rising to any challenging occasion, much less one as loaded with as many demanding issues as I faced after Bert's death, which had to be resolved.

I was essentially on my own for the first time.

My parents, older brother and I had lived a life managed by our wonderful housekeeper, who resided with us. My every wish was her pleasure to fulfil. I floated through childhood deliriously happy, spoiled and secure without any responsibilities or tasks to perform.

My only challenges began at age eleven. My father's business suffered a massive decline and my mother had to return to teaching to help provide financial support for the family. By that time, I knew nothing about preparing meals, doing laundry or cleaning our home. My limited contributions were hit and miss and came when we no longer could afford help to run our house.

By the time I was married, I learned on the job about the rudimentary tasks of digging into housekeeping. However, I became much more accomplished during my six years of teaching in Cheltenham Township secondary schools, reaping many accolades for my work. When our children arrived, I learned how to reign in four sons and worked diligently to teach them helpful tasks so our family could function cooperatively. Bert and I fashioned a family culture raising responsible, helpful, loving sons, following in his family tradition, not mine.

So just how did I develop the "blood and guts" to rise to the challenges following Bert's death? I learned quickly that achieving acclaim for parental prowess was nowhere near enough to enable me to handle the urgent, extreme pressures I managed to surmount, with help from many experts, of course.

I certainly didn't learn from my early life training and a lack of trial and error so necessary to build the fortitude needed as a single mother of four testosterone-fueled boys.

Believe me, I had my fair share of "Aha" moments.

THE JOYS OF CARPENTER STREET
&
TALES OF
CHILDHOOD

My Own Private "Disneyland"

WAY BACK IN THE OLDEN DAYS of the 1940s, before television, kids like me found many ways to amuse ourselves. Inclement or cold weather found us meeting at each other's homes and playing board games like Monopoly or someone's newest birthday-present game. Of course, our first choice was running around outside, mixing it up with our neighborhood gang.

Picture a tree lined street of 23 semi-detached homes on the even numbered side of the street facing odd numbered homes on the other side. Inside these 46 houses lived at least 50 children, ranging in age from toddlers through high school.

Our block also boasted a wide street, which became our stomping ground after dinner, when traffic was nil, signaling it was time for *Hide and Seek*, our favorite activity, which welcomed kids of all ages. We played every summer evening until it got too dark to locate who we were seeking. The older kids on our team orchestrated our strategies for success by planning escape routes through certain bushes. They would pop in and out of boundary lines and demonstrate how to skip from tree to tree to escape detection.

We became experts at avoiding capture. The only thing that suspended this evening ritual was when we departed for our annual "down the shore" trip to escape the heat of summer.

Hopscotch was another favorite game and a particular female specialty. We chalked the outline of numbered squares on the pavement for continual use and worked hard to jump into these spaces without stepping on any lines. The key feature of the game was the special individualized "pad" each player would use to claim a numbered spot by throwing it onto the areas numbered 1 to 10 on the outlined form.

Every girl fancied her own special pad, which she skipped to retrieve and bring back home without any missteps on the drawn lines. The pride of ingenuity in using keys, toys or weights, which wouldn't roll on a line but plop right in a numbered square to mark your goal, was high. Your favorite pad was waiting there to be retrieved for the homeward return trip and then it was returned to your pocket.

Our troop of girls also loved swaying to the movement of *Jump Rope*. We always rotated rope-turners, so that everyone got a chance to jump. As we bounced in the air over the turning rope, we all invariably recited a funny rhyme or counted what number we could attain until we were tripped by the rope, which ended our turn.

As competent as I was with a single turning rope, I never mastered *Double Dutch*, which meant the rope-turner held a rope end in each hand, which she turned, forming a double strand for a contestant to jump over. This was no easy task.

"Janet, step in now," Rita implored, as both hands rotated the ropes for my jumping turn.

"Oh, no, I missed again," I moaned, as the minute I jumped in between the rotating double strands, I got tangled. This was beyond my athletic potential, so I was always relegated to sit on the pavement, watching the other stars easily handle the sideways rope momentum.

The highlight of our outdoor activities was when we travelled to the middle of the block to watch the older boys play *Territory*. We all clustered around a mud bank where a tree had been many years before and gazed in amazement at the teenagers who were carving up their newly won land. Proudly displaying their precious varied pen knives, they took turns throwing them in the hard ground to create their own distinct territory. Although we were amazed to imagine our parents allowing our brothers to play with penknives, I don't remember ever seeing a drop of spilled blood or hearing about any incident involving any cuts. Those guys were deft.

The boys in our gang scheduled regular baseball and football games in the street, which easily bored us girls because they were so frequent. We paid little attention to their athletic prowess in these activities, as we were never good enough to participate with them.

Our Carpenter Street gang was even entertained by animals, which strolled regularly down our street. Once a week, trash trucks, which were essentially enormous open bins on wheels, filed down the street, drawn by a team of horses. Of course, we were used to seeing working horses, as our milk bottles were delivered with horse-drawn wagons.

But it was only before I started elementary school that I ever had a chance to feed the trash-truck horses, because they came in the morning. The milk wagons came even earlier in the morning, when I was usually still dreaming about finally conquering *Double Dutch*.

When the trash-collectors emptied our cans, the wagons stopped, and the men paused to help us feed apples to the horses. For a kid my age, that thrill was unimaginable and beat any experience, at least until our most famous animal arrived.

The best treat was the Knife Sharpener Man, who came to our neighborhood every few months, accompanied by a real, live monkey! He played an organ-grinder to arouse the homeowners' attention and set up shop in front of a home in the middle of the block, ready for business. The crowd grew larger by the minute as mothers and children gathered around, thoroughly enraptured by the sight of a small monkey. We were in heaven, watching sparks fly from the sharpening wheel and a moment later, a dancing monkey.

Then there was the Joel B. Goleman's *Surgical Special Sideshow*, a special production by my older brother, who operated on frogs he had captured from nearby Cobbs Creek Parkway. After chloroforming them on our front landing, he meticulously used his chemistry set scalpel (after all, he was already an expert knife thrower from the

Territory games) to expose the beating heart of the frog to the mesmerized crowd.

They would gladly have paid more than the ten-cent price of admission (the cost of a mere comic book), to see this show. I coughed from inhaling the chloroform fumes as I collected exhibit fees for him.

These Carpenter Street outdoor experiences were not only fun; they provided all of us with a golden education. The sports competitions, the camaraderie mixing with varied age groups, and the games we invented taught us socialization skills we utilized throughout our "wonder years" and likely informed the type of parents we became.

Our generation did just fine without any televisions, computers or cell phones, the devices our grandchildren now devour like candy. In fact, I believe we probably had more fun than kids do today. When I watch them content to be isolated with their techie tools as they sit next to each other and text each other, I wonder how much they would do that if they knew there was a hot game of *Hide and Seek* happening right outside their house.

What we children experienced with our older and younger neighbors was something special, as I look back on it through the lens of today's kids.

We made many friendships among our gang members, enhanced our listening skills as we gathered to follow radio show adventures, and enhanced our motor skills each day from all the physical activity we enjoyed.

All in all, in the best way, my neighborhood was my own personal Disneyland.

Eddie Goldman Learns to Fight

I DON'T KNOW WHICH WAS NOISIER back when my father was growing up—the city of Philadelphia or the inside of his house.

"Children! Hush up!"

"Herman, Cele, Fay, Eddie, Gert, Sy—stop fighting in here! You're making so much noise I almost didn't hear the doorbell ring. Get out of the living room, right now."

Sarah collected herself and greeted the visitor as she opened the door.

"Hello, can I help you?"

"Does Joseph Goldman live here?"

"Yes," Sarah said. "He's not here right now, but he'll be home soon. Who shall I say came to see him?"

"I'm Ida, his wife from Russia, and these are my six children."

"Oh, my God!"

Two wives from the same man?

How could that happen?

I first heard about this convoluted drama many years later as the child of one of those children, who happened to be my father.

Apparently, according to family folklore, the story goes that my grandfather, Joseph, upon learning that his Russian wife discovered his whereabouts in Salem, Massachusetts, ran away from both wives and eleven children.

That story endured within my family until four years ago when I took a genealogy course at Cheltenham Adult School. That's when I discovered a second cousin, once removed, who was a real ancestry buff. Steven Heberman, the great-grandson of my grandmother, Sarah Goldman's sister, Rose (are you following this?), provided many revealing documents about dear Grandpop, which cleared away any existent cobwebs passed down from one generation to the next.

First, I heard about an article from 1909 in a Salem newspaper, describing Martha Lieberman Goldman's support action against Joseph Goldman for failure to pay child and spousal support for herself and her five children, who apparently had just emigrated from Russia.

Then I received the 1910 Census Report from Philadelphia, documenting Joseph and Sarah Goldman's residence. Did they flee Massachusetts to avoid support obligations? This news was followed by the 1920 Census Report, demonstrating that my father, Edward Edwin Goldman, and his five siblings still lived with their parents by the time my father was thirteen. By now, all my fictionalized imaginative stories about my grandfather, Joseph, had factually evaporated.

What topped off reality was the 1925 *Philadelphia Inquirer* news article about a court decision awarding my grandmother, Sarah, $5,000 and her daughter, my Aunt Faye, $10,000 ($140,00 in current value) for injuries they sustained when a truck collided with the trolley they were riding.

Actually, this unbelievable series of events did not end there. The shocking tales of disbelief continued!

One of Sarah and Joseph's daughters, Celia, married Nathan Bernstein. Their daughter, Lois, married Murray Goldman in 1950. If that last name sounds familiar, you're up to speed. Murray just happened to be the son of Joseph Goldman's Russian son, Samuel. The picture is complete once you understand that the grandchild of Joseph's American wife married the grandson of his Russian wife! The young blissful couple ventured out to California, where Murray Goldman pursued his career.

In California, Lois Goldman, Joseph's granddaughter, reconnected with Evelyn Litvin Polack, who was my mother, Esther Litvin Goleman's niece. Evelyn was raised by her grandparents, Molly and Abe Litvin, following the death of her mother during childbirth. The two girls met each other at family events at Eddie and Esther Goleman's home while they were growing up, as they were the respective nieces of the couple.

Get ready for one last shock, I promise.

When Lois died in the late eighties, Evelyn and Murray became a couple and married in 1991. My brother, Joel, his daughter, Myla, and I attended their wedding in Van Nuys, California, to cheer on the happy couple.

What's most unique about this tale of shocking revelations and surprises is that my father, Eddie Goleman, never mentioned any details to my brother or me about his childhood "families." It took more than seventy years to unravel my paternal family history through the dedicated efforts of distant relatives who tracked me down to share this compelling story.

Grandpop Joseph, our favorite family "villain," died in 1928, and his funeral was attended by *both* sets of his progeny, American and Russian, when it was held in Philadelphia.

All of those shenanigans played a role in my father's adventures growing up in a one-parent family. When Eddie's father concluded his second disappearing act, he left two wives and twelve children to fend for themselves in America.

It wasn't easy for my father. Bigotry and intolerance came with the territory.

"Get off my corner, Jew-boy."

"Yeah, sure, you and who else are going to make me, Big Shot?"

"This is my spot for selling papers, and you ain't gonna cut in."

"You've never been here at 5:30 before and I've been here all week, so move on!"

"Come on boys, let's show this kid who's running this paper route!"

Eddie, formally known as Edward E. Goldman, didn't win this fight, as the score was three to one in the other kid's favor. A team of six fists left his face bloodied and his stomach pummeled. He managed to make his way home, where his mother found him.

"Oh, my God, Eddie, what happened to your face?"

"I don't feel too good, Mom. I got into a fight with some kids over the route and they stole all my papers and I don't have any money for the milk this morning."

"Sit down, so I can wash your bloody face. You're staying home from school, today, that's for sure."

The only upside to my father's frequent street bouts was the experience he gained defending himself from the neighborhood onslaught of anti-Semitic aggression. To help his five siblings and six stepsisters and brothers support their family, he did any odd jobs he could find, before and after school. His first discretionary spending was the purchase of boxing gloves to help him develop what became his defense mechanism to survive his teenage years.

"Mr. DiSantis, I have a deal to present to you," said my father on his first day at the gym.

"I'm Eddie Goldman and I want to work at the Ace Boxing Ring. I'll do any chores that need doing in exchange for a chance to watch the pros work out and practice."

"What can you do, kid? Have you ever worked for a cleaning service? Can you scrub toilets and floors and wash dishes?"

Eddie had it all figured out.

"I'll do whatever you need from six to 10 p.m., three nights a week so I can learn the ropes about boxing. You see, it's my dream to compete in the Golden Gloves tournament and I need some knowhow."

"You sound like a real hustler, kid. I'll take a chance and see how hard you work to keep this place clean. You look okay, so call me Mr. D. I'll give you a shot starting tomorrow."

"Thanks, thanks so much Mr. D., you won't regret it."

Eddie's career at Central High School in Philadelphia was fraught with frustration because he had little time for studies. His day started at five to get ready to sell papers before school and concluded when he finished his homework at midnight. In between, he worked at a grocery store after school and spent three nights a week cleaning whatever Mr. D. told him to do inside the Ace Boxing Ring.

His teachers weren't exactly thrilled.

"Mr. Goldman, I'm expecting better grades from you. You barely passed this history exam. I know you have the ability and I am suspecting you're too lazy. I even caught you napping in class the other day."

"Sorry, Professor, but I didn't have a chance to study much yesterday, I had to work overtime. I really like to hear your lectures about the Greek and Roman empires and the weapons they used to wage war. I really do."

"I'm glad something is getting your attention, young man, because you are beginning to become a disappointment to me. You're not the only one who is working hard to make money for your family, so stop making excuses and do something about making a mark in your classes."

"Thanks, Professor, for taking an interest in me and spending the time talking to me. I'll work harder, I promise."

Although his marks weren't stellar, Eddie was able to graduate in the top quarter of Central High's class and earn a Baccalaureate Degree. He even enrolled in a college-level evening course to pursue a degree in business.

All that effort didn't escape his older brother, Hank.

"Eddie, I have a great idea about our new company name. Instead of using our last name twice, how about if you change the spelling of your name to Goleman and then the firm name would be Goldman & Goleman. That way, it wouldn't be so conspicuous that we're brothers. What do you think?"

"Hey, Hank, in the game of life you always taught me that the older brother rules. If you think that would look better for our business, I don't mind changing one little letter in my last name. It might even make my name stand out when I'm in the ring for one of my amateur fights. I'm all in with the idea."

Eddie and Hank formed Goldman & Goleman, a partnership to sell construction materials, and Eddie went on the road to perfect his sales skills. The company lasted a few years before the brothers parted ways to engage in different businesses. By then, the "e" remained in Eddie's last name and he was a Goleman forever.

Eddie's amateur boxing career, commenced in the streets of Strawberry Mansion, played out for a few years in competitive bouts. The professionals at the boxing ring took him under their wing, offering encouragement and training tips and they essentially adopted him as their mascot. But once Eddie became serious about his romantic relationship with Esther Litvin, his boxing aspirations quickly vanished.

"Es, I've decided to hang up my boxing gloves," he told her. "After all, I'm not going to become a professional boxer."

"Gee, Eddie, you were having such success in the ring with all your wins."

"Yes, but I have to concentrate on my business, especially now that we're making serious plans and you've agreed to go steady with me. In a few more years I'll have this business going really well and we can plan to get married."

"Wow, is that a tough decision for you to make?"

"It's no contest between my two careers, because you are the real prize I want."

"That sounds so good! I'm blushing, Eddie."

"I love you Hon, so keep blushing!"

One thing led to another, and Eddie and Esther got married and started a family. My father, who grew up in such a bustling neighborhood, became involved in many local activities, and one of his biggest passions developed on the golf courses of suburban Philadelphia.

"Eddie, our gang needs your support," one of his pals told him one day, "and as a knock-golfer, you fit right in our picture. We want to start a golf club and have the property all picked out in Conshohocken. We even have a name: Green Valley Country Club."

"Joe, I'm flattered you thought of me. What are you looking for?"

"We need your commitment for a sum of money, which will entitle you to become a Charter Member of the club and serve on the Board of Directors."

"I'm interested as long as there is a payout period to fulfill my commitment, because I'm somewhat tight right now."

"Good enough, I'll have my lawyer contact you to draw up the papers tomorrow."

"It's a deal, Joe. Let's shake on it."

Eddie, already an expert golfer, thrived at Green Valley Country Club and played the course twice every weekend. The entire family enjoyed Sunday dinners at the club, after the children participated in activities geared for their respective ages and Esther finished her round of golf with friends.

Eddie, always fueled by energy and ambition, replaced his Golden Glove aspirations with the golden golf balls he won as a champion at the club. He continued his pursuit of chasing balls on the links for the next thirty years but never compromised his commitment to family.

Raised by Russians

MY MOTHER, ESTHER LITVIN, was raised by Russian immigrants in a house located behind the family store at Second and Girard in Philadelphia. Although they enjoyed financial security, bordering on relative luxury, Esther's family experienced tragic losses that impacted everyone.

Still, my mother seemed to have unbridled enthusiasm for getting a good education and expanding her horizons beyond the neighborhood. She was particularly excited about her high school senior class trip to Washington, D.C.

"Mother, the President was so patient as the long line of my classmates moved forward, one at a time, so that each one of us could shake his hand."

"Did your principal introduce you to him, Esther? Did you practice good manners? Were you polite?"

"Yes, Mother, to all of your questions, yes, yes, yes, and President Harding smiled so sincerely when he greeted me with 'How do you do, Miss Litvin?' There I was, on my senior class trip to Washington, standing in the White House, touching the President's hand. I'll never forget it, ever and I certainly won't wash my hand!"

"You are such a lucky girl, Esther; now go see if you can help Father in the store with the cash register."

My mother bounced along from our house through the connecting door to find her father inside *A. Litvin's Leather Goods* store, where she would help count change or whatever else Abe needed. By 1926, he had established a prosperous leather business supplying raw materials to shoemakers throughout the city. To his immigrant community, Abe had "made it in America."

"Esther," her father said, "you're back just in time to take the broom and do a little housekeeping because Hilda went home sick today and didn't clean the house or the store."

"Sure, Father, shall I also feed the dogs or did one of my sisters do it already?"

"I think Rose or Ethyl might have. It's funny not to count on Jeannie working here, now that she's a married lady and moved in with her husband."

"Father, how come my brother doesn't do much around here to help? He's so busy taking horseback riding lessons, he's never in the store when you need him."

"Enough of that Miss, get busy. By the way, don't do anything to upset your mother because tomorrow is too difficult for her. It's the memorial date of your brother Sammy's death and she's very upset already."

"Please don't worry Father, we'll all be very careful to care for her. Wait until I tell you later what happened to me on my class trip and who I met in Washington!"

"Let's be sure you do that as soon as we get a chance."

A few days later, Esther approached her parents with her idea of how to resolve the big decision, which had been hanging over the family.

"Mother and Father, I've made up my mind about teacher's college. You don't have to pay any money to send me the University of Pennsylvania, because I'll be just as happy to go to Philadelphia Normal School. There's no tuition to pay there to study to become a teacher, so just look at what you'll be saving."

"Esther, are you sure you'll get as good a teaching education there?"

"Mother, don't worry, my high school teachers have assured me about the quality of education there and a few of my friends are attending Normal School, too.

"Will you be happy enough there?" said Abe.

"Please don't think any more about it. I'll be a great teacher and make them proud as their graduate. I'm so appreciative of you taking care of me for another two years. Just think, my two sisters are planning to go right out to work and earn a salary right after their high school commercial course. I'm continuing with my education because of *your* support. You're now looking at a prospective Philadelphia Normal School graduate!"

True to her word, Esther Litvin excelled in school and fulfilled her prophesy of being well prepared to teach in the Philadelphia School District, where she began her career.

She also had the good taste to develop a relationship with Edward E. Goleman (formally Goldman), which led to their engagement and marriage a few years after graduating.

"Mother, pleassssse, you have to change your mind!" said Esther one day, reacting to her mother's stubbornness about having her future son's mother chauffeured to the wedding. "Eddie's mother, Sarah, insists you should send a car to bring her to our wedding! She's making him miserable by creating such a fuss about a personal driver and he is so embarrassed about asking you!"

"Esther, that is unreasonable. I have too much on my mind the night before your wedding to appease a stubborn lady at this last minute."

What's a girl to do with two stubborn matriarchs?

"Mother, we're frantic because she even threatened not to come! What if she doesn't appear? You just have to do something!"

"What a beginning for good relations between families! All right, Esther, I'll make new arrangements. Isn't it enough I had to plan for transporting Eddie's five siblings when his mother was going with her brother? Just promise me that you won't say a word of this to your father. I can't handle getting him excited!"

My mother's wedding had everyone emotional, especially her own mother.

"Oh, Esther, every time, I think about your three-year-old niece, Evelyn, as your flower girl, my heart breaks from sobbing for her mother, my Jeannie, who is no longer alive! I need strength to get through your wedding without more to worry about!"

"Oh, thanks so much, Mother. I'll love you forever and always be here to help you!"

The wedding went off without a hitch and Esther settled into married life quite nicely, along with continuing her teaching career. That didn't last for terribly long, as Esther retired from the classroom with the birth of her first son, Joel, and five years later, her life became even fuller with the birth of a new daughter, Janet, who would become me.

My appearance prompted a move to a bigger home.

"Eddie," my mother said, "are you sure we can really afford the big house with four bedrooms at 62nd and Carpenter?"

"Es, stop worrying. We've gone over the figures so many times. Joel and the baby will each have their own bedrooms and Alvina will have the bedroom in the rear."

The housekeeper needed her own room, for sure.

"Do we really need the apartment in New York city to entertain clients? Isn't that extra financial pressure? "

Apparently, my father had everything under control. I didn't notice. I only had food and crawling on my mind.

"Remember, Hon, I'm sharing the expenses there with my partners. Stop worrying! I worked out the numbers too many times for it not to work."

"You're sure, right? Can we definitely swing it? I'm concerned."

"Honey, everything will be fine; trust me."

"Eddie, you know I'm such a wreck with my father's passing this year after losing my sister last year. She was only 22, Eddie. This wasn't supposed to happen."

"Esther, I'm here to make sure our family is safe in our new home. Imagine, living near Cobbs Creek Park. It's a great place. Okay, dear?"

"If you say so, Eddie, if you say so."

In the ensuing years, Esther enjoyed a rather carefree life golfing at a country club and engaging in charitable organizations, as her children attended school during the day. The housekeeper handled the management of the house and cooked for the family. The only exception? My mother made jelly rolls for dessert. Besides that, her main job was assuming the role of disciplinarian for one of her two children, as she couldn't quite catch the other one (me) to reinforce her authority.

"Janet Sondra, get right over here," she'd snarl, her face contorted into a tight, menacing stare, which always seem to have the desired effect.

"Okay," I'd wail, only what I said under my breath was quite different. "Do I have to? Why can't I run the other way, just like my brother does?"

By that point, my tears had become plentiful as I slowly trudged forward to collect my just punishment, which were usually slaps on my backside.

"Mommy," I'd hiccup, "I didn't mean to puncture the sides of the new ice bucket with the ice pick. I was just trying to chop up the ice."

There was no protestation or wails of "sorry" that could mitigate the spanking I invariably suffered! Nor did my sobbing deter Mom's determination to mete out the punishment for my latest criminal act.

"Oh, if only I had the guts of my brother, Joel!"

"That's the end of your career of selling lemonade at the curb, Janet Sondra. Now just pack right up this instant!"

That was the end of that, and my future as an entrepreneur was nipped in the bud.

After the end of World War II, Eddie's business faltered, and he was forced to close his metal goods foundry and offices. For years, his company manufactured war materials, which had enabled him to obtain supplies of gasoline to drive to the office every day. The success of the business enabled our family to enjoy an easy lifestyle during difficult times.

Soon after 1945 came to an end, it became Eddie's family's turn to experience hardships. Esther stepped up to the bat and enlisted in her own family's war effort, to help keep it afloat. Without hesitating, she returned to her earlier vocation of teaching school and handled all the challenges that came with such a momentous change in her life. She earned her husband's and children's undying admiration and love for this abrupt turn-about she performed in her life.

A Temporary Juvenile Delinquent

LIKE MOST CHILDREN, I learned the difference between right and wrong, what was acceptable behavior and what was not, from parents, an older sibling, housekeepers, friends and teachers.

However, in second grade I ran into an unexpected challenge, in the form of the Ten Commandments, "Thou shalt not steal," to be exact.

Undeterred, I commenced my criminal conduct without any formal training.

On a fateful Monday morning, my teacher, Miss Soffin, made an announcement.

"Listen up everyone, we're making a new formation when we line up. Starting today, we'll file behind my desk, in front of the blackboard, to leave our classroom."

At lunch and after school dismissal, we lined up accordingly to march out into the school yard in this new world order.

One day, as I was the last one in line, I spotted a collection of brightly colored rubber erasers beckoning me from a partially opened drawer in Miss Soffin's desk. Clustered in a pile and tightly squeezed in a corner, they appeared so inviting. After quickly perusing my location and the proximity and angle of my teacher's view, I reached in and removed a few of those colored, squeezy delights and marched out triumphantly.

Seeing as I was one of the taller gals in my class, I had no difficulty positioning myself at the end of the departure line. Throughout my escapade, which featured the excitement of escaping detection, I never contemplated the effects of stealing from my teacher. I also ignored any thought of what it would mean to face the music in case I were caught in the act. Obviously, I didn't have any prior experience in the felony department, so I didn't worry about any such event or its consequences.

By the time a couple of weeks had passed, I had pilfered my own collection of lost erasers, which I had conveniently rediscovered. I kept my loot neatly secreted and piled in a section of one of my bedroom bureau drawers, safe and sound I thought, until that fateful day.

"Janet, I put some socks away in your drawer and saw a bunch of erasers," my mom said one day, taking me totally by surprise. "Where did they come from?"

I didn't miss a beat.

"Oh, my friends gave them to me." I said, barely audible, as I was ready to faint.

In that moment, I began to recognize the black specter of fear closing in on me. I wasn't sure what to do, as my breathing was suddenly becoming tight.

"How did you get so many?"

I shrugged.

"Which friends were giving away their erasers?"

Half shrug.

"What's going on, here?"

I had no shrugs left. I was trapped and as my body shook, tears spontaneously appeared, leading to heaving body sobs and a bunch blubbering, in audible excuses, until I could catch my breath enough to speak.

"Mom, I took them from Miss Soffin's desk."

I couldn't believe I had actually said it out loud.

"You did what?" she shrieked.

My head hung in front of me like an overripe tomato.

"I can't believe you would do such a bad thing to your teacher and shame your family, too. Well, young lady, you'll just have to bring Miss Soffin's erasers right back to her tomorrow and tell her what a mistake you made."

"Yes, Mother," I mumbled, between sobs.

"Whatever prompted you to do such a wicked thing?"

I shrugged my shoulders, crying inconsolably, feeling upset, embarrassed and guilty, after confessing to my act of thievery and falling out of grace with my mother. I shuddered to think how embarrassed I would feel confessing to my teacher when I returned the treasure trove of erasers the next day. Facing the potential repercussions of what I had done was an overwhelming burden. I could only hope that a full confession and apology might provide salvation and hopefully maintain my classroom reputation.

Who would have thought I would become a juvenile delinquent at such an early age, seven to be exact? Luckily, I entered rehab just as suddenly. After a sleepless night, I began the next day to put my own creative strategy into play. Each afternoon, and for many others thereafter, I returned my loot a few at a time at dismissal, the same way I had secreted stolen them before. Silently, at the end of our exit line, I deposited a few purloined erasers back into Miss Soffin's desk drawer.

My unique criminal activity went miraculously undetected by my teacher and escaped any further inspection from my mother. Once I had returned my treasured bounty, I abruptly terminated my streak of juvenile delinquency and promised myself that I would never engage in such a despicable act again.

As a further act of contrition, I volunteered to wash the blackboards after school for about a month. Sometimes, I wondered if Miss Soffin would guess why I suddenly jumped in to do this classroom housekeeping, while at the same time her missing pile of erasers mysteriously filled her drawer again.

I was proud of how I resolved my problem and saved my reputation in the classroom. However, I restrained myself from revealing my selfish master plan to my mother, as that was clearly the best way to avoid punishment.

After reading my latest report card, which included Miss Soffin's positive comments about my volunteer efforts in class, Mother seemed pleased.

"Isn't Miss Soffin gracious with her forgiveness?"

I nodded.

This deviation so early in life from "the right path" set a high standard for my corrected behavior heading into the future.

I never looked back on my wayward ways, as I became whisked along a path of receiving many accolades during my numerous roles as a student leader.

My Wild, Wooly Brother

WHEN IT CAME TO MY OLDER BROTHER, Joel, I always heard my mother refer to the challenge of "managing" him, as if he were a project, and I never understood why she felt that way.

Joel needed surgery when he was an infant and as a result he was spoiled by both parents until he began to run amuck and stopped seeking their approval for his creative activities. According to Mom, he was "always into something" and was obsessed with exploring, experimenting and following his hunches to seek excursions. As a child, he was like a big game hunter because of his fascination with animals and critters that others wouldn't dream of touching, much less capturing.

One summer, while we were staying at our summer rental home in Ventnor, New Jersey, he wandered off one day to the bay area, several blocks away. Although he was only around ten or eleven years old, he thought nothing of going fishing for some eels. Who even knew eels existed before his foray into the wild to seek these strange sea creatures? After he was gone so long that my mom was ready to call the police, Joel returned home with a large pail of swarming, slithering, wormy, black fish, if you could call them that.

"Just what in the world do you think you're going to do with a bucket full of eels?" Mom, said, or should I say, screamed.

"Mom, don't you want to know the cool way I caught them?"

"Absolutely, no! I'm not interested, Joel, and I'm going to walk you back to the bay area right this minute so you can throw them back into the water."

"But, Mom, I want to cook them for a dinner!"

"We're leaving this minute, so pick up that pail! Janet, you hurry up, too. Wait until your father hears about this newest trick!"

I was fascinated but grossed out. Wherever Joel had learned about cooking eels remains a deep secret, even to this day.

Once Mom and Dad sent Joel to Camp Saginaw in the Pocono Mountains, summers turned into an eight-week vacation for my parents. They rented a house on the shore and Dad the joined Mom and me every weekend for his escape "down the shore." When it was just me and her, she seemed so relaxed, relieved from the constant challenges of keeping up with Joel's adventures and his creative journeys around our neighborhood on his bike. While Joel was having supervised fun at his overnight camp, Mom enjoyed her ultimate vacation.

We reunited as a family of four for the final two weeks of summer. During that time, Joel and I learned how to get used to each other again. He put up with my incessant questions and I acclimated myself to his barrage of "brotherly" punches.

There were times when he actually asked for my assistance to help plan and execute an activity After all, I was his assistant who collected 10 cents from each person in the crowd that gathered at our front steps to watch him lord over a bunch of huge frogs from Cobbs Creek Park.

Because Joel was five years older than I, we really didn't play around much together. As a matter of fact, the older he got, the more fun he had with me—at my expense. He made a steady habit of embarrassing me when he was with his friends. When I was in junior high, I idolized those older high school boys and enjoyed hanging around when they congregated at our home. That is, until Joel chased me away. The boys took turns playing cards at each other's homes and in our house, Joel performed the ultimate trick on me.

One night, I was perched quietly on the windowsill, watching their card game. While the cards were being shuffled, Joel walked out for a few minutes. He pranced back proudly into the room, parading around with one of my new 32AA bras, (the smallest size) on his sleeve, which I had just purchased that day. I almost fainted, while the gang let out hoops of laughter as I scampered away as fast as I could.

I must admit it. I hung around Joel almost as much as possible, pestering him for attention. Usually, he reached a moment where he would take what he called "a friendly swing" at me, at which point I would go yelling to Mom.

"Joel, just hit me!"

"Joel, leave her alone or your father will definitely hear about this."

During one of my "hovering" moments, while Joel was doing his homework at the dining room table, he jabbed at me with his pencil point. This was different from our other altercations. I stared at my left underarm where I saw a black mark which had broken through my skin to leave an indelible, imbedded dot. This was serious business and my mom didn't hesitate to call Doctor Abe Levin, our family friend, to see me right away as an official emergency.

This after-hours office visit involved a surgical procedure where he made a large incision and scraped out the dot of pencil lead to prevent any possible poisoning. I was terrified throughout this entire episode until I realized the glorious punishment that would be meted out to Joel for stabbing me "when Dad got home."

Our perpetual episodes of sibling escapades and occasional torture ultimately evolved into a loving, respected relationship.

Joel was the most brilliant, interesting, multi-faceted collector I have ever met. No matter what he subjected me to as his younger sister, it was somehow okay because he was just being Joel.

Esther Goleman Teaches Me a Lesson

I HAD NO IDEA WHAT A LUCKY BABY I was when I selected Esther and Eddie Goleman to become my parents on October 27th in what became a magical year for all of us. How could I have ever recognized or appreciated the special benefits of spending my childhood summers in rented homes at the shore or later at overnight camps, meeting Dad every Sunday for dinner with Mom and Joel after his outings at Green Valley Country Club, or reveling in the tender care provided by Alvina, our family "concierge," who handled our household so that none of us ever had a care in the world.

But all good things must come to an end. In our case, a series of events unfolded in rapid succession when I was eleven years old, imploding our idyllic life. First, our beloved Alvina departed from our home to pursue a new career as a factory worker.

Then, Dad's manufacturing business floundered from a rapid over-expansion from its war production, which caused a dramatic shutdown.

Dad suffered emotionally and couldn't find suitable work. Mom rose up heroically to fend off the sudden economic hardship thrust upon us by getting her teaching certification reinstated and going back to work. Her challenge became balancing the hour-long drive each way to a school in another section of the city, let alone stepping up to become the chef and manager of our home.

I was faced with the unprecedented challenge of becoming a real contributing member of our household. Me, the pampered kid who never lifted a finger to assist in any household function and lacked experiential know-how in every area of housekeeping, faced many new trials and tribulations.

In the middle of this chaotic turmoil, I inherited a new bedroom. I went from the small bedroom next to my parents to Alvina's large rear bedroom, complete with mirrored double-doored closets and twin beds.

Under ordinary circumstances, I would have been in heaven, with my new accessibility to dancing in my new bedroom every minute I could. Just to watch my body movement reflected in mirrors all around me would have normally filled me to the brim with pleasure.

But under our new circumstances and my newly prescribed workload, I focused more on envisioning myself being turned back into a fairy tale princess, who no longer needed to do her share of work to keep our home in order.

Where was the Disney life I had enjoyed as a younger girl?

Much to my surprise, facing these new challenges and learning how to help my parents offered the greatest lessons I could learn as I entered my teenage years. I reluctantly became Mom's backup, assisting with housework chores, from the simple act of hanging up my own clothes (imagine that!) to vacuuming carpets and sponging linoleum floors.

What a great leap of faith for such a spoiled child.

I learned my first dramatic lesson in empathy by watching my exhausted mother master her own learning curve of housekeeping survival. Knowing I was relieving her of some effort gave me my first taste of comforting others and the beginning of a sense of maturity.

Let's be honest, though. We didn't rough it too badly, as in hanging towels and sheets outside in the winter to dry on clotheslines and collect them as frozen, stiff boards, as Alvina had always done. Thankfully, we succumbed to a clothes dryer, which helped make laundry duty easier for all.

Mom's newly forged role as a heroine served as my personal model when thirty years later, my own immediate family imploded.

How fortunate that training proved to be, that I had Mom as my example for how to step up to the plate just when it was required most.

Unbeknownst to me, this most valuable lesson of my life, watching my mom assume and thrive with her new responsibilities, remained tucked away until I really needed it.

Ultimately, Dad found supervisory work in a commercial construction business. Mom was transferred to teach in a school in our own neighborhood, and they were able to hire a housekeeper to manage the daily chores, which were necessary to run our house.

Once again, I was back in Disneyland in the privacy of my bedroom.

Carolina Summer

While en route to the lush Carolina mountains
for a summer camp job,
the hum of the train skimming the tracks
provided a cadence as I practiced
repeating my monotonous mantra:
"I'm *six* teen, *six* teen, *six* teen"
although I wasn't.

I crept off at the third station stop
and was welcomed to the south when I
bumped into a fountain marked
"For Coloreds Only."

Flustered, I ran back to the safety of my seat.
expecting to play with kids at sports.
I shoveled scraps from dishes, not home plate,
and swabbed the planked cabin floors.
I saved mopping toilet bowls for last
while plotting my escape.

Days off in a hick town altered plans.
Swaying in the rear of an open-back truck,

REINVENTING MYSELF

squashed against other counselors,
I was transported over the line
to the hypocrisy of southern life.

The locals taught me how to tap,
and dance steps morphed into clogging
at spontaneous street dance rallies.
I became a born-again redneck
while singing, "Nothing could be finer..."

In eight weeks, I grew those two years,
cleaned up kids, played with them, too,
and stretched my words into a spongy drawl
when melting into town on escape trips,
not learning until years later,
that I missed my chance
to bump into Thomas Wolfe.

What Doesn't Kill You, Makes You Stronger

THROUGHOUT MY ELEMENTARY SCHOOL years, my road to leadership was built upon hard work, support for classmates and volunteerism, which began in second grade when I began cleaning blackboard erasers to atone for my sin of stealing erasers from Miss Soffin's desk. I didn't know it at the time, but this was my first foray into politics. After that, I was always elected whenever I entered a competition for a leadership role.

By the time I graduated from Sayre Junior High School, I was elected treasurer of the entire school. I had no idea that this job would entail hand-stamping my name 937 times on each student's identification card that I proudly distributed.

My leadership horizon expanded at West Philadelphia High School when I was elected Grade Director four years in a row to represent my class on the Student Government Board. I honed new popularity skills as I expanded my circle of friends and provided help whenever I saw an opportunity. This all felt natural to me at the time. After serving as a cafeteria aide, who helped straighten tables and chairs for lunch groups, I was promoted to a committee, which planned fund-raising activities for our class. I even started a social club for neighborhood girlfriends, which met each Friday night for fun and games.

By the time I graduated from high school, I was the female Senior Grade Director who also performed in the chorus line of our school shows.

Graduation night became my personal Academy Awards ceremony as I received the notorious Gift of Roses. Each girl graduate removed one rose from her bouquet and passed it along the rows to be collected and presented to me for my service to the school. I was also the designated recipient of the History Prize and won a scholarship to the University of Pennsylvania, which made my parents particularly proud.

Since we graduated in in January, we had little time between the exhilaration of partying and preparing to embark on our adventures as mid-year college freshmen.

Emotionally, we flip-flopped from feeling like "kings of the walk" to insecure novices discovering a campus, buying required textbooks, learning which buildings housed our classrooms, and the routes to find them. We laughed, comparing our new college experience to the insecure first days in kindergarten.

"Will I find a friend? How do I find my way?"

We were so thankful that all of our adjustments were made on a campus in our own city, compared to the additional strain of learning about a new locale.

In our class yearbook, I had been pictured along with a male classmate as "Most Likely to Succeed." During my early time at Penn, the success continued as I took a leadership role in many activities on campus. My classmates expected it of me, and I delivered, at least until the day I ran into a highly unexpected rejection. This "tragedy" occurred soon after we settled into a routine of classes and orienting ourselves on campus.

Sorority Rush time!

I felt fortunate that of the eight high school classmates admitted with me to Penn, one of them, Naomi, was a best friend. She and I locked arms and faced the new music together as we threw our names into the ring to "rush" D Phi E, short for Delta Phi Epsilon.

The process included various social events where we met potential sorority sisters and hopefully made a positive enough impression to be invited to join their group. Notification on that decision was to come by retrieving an envelope bearing your name at a designated student center.

That morning, inside the Phi Epsilon Pi mailroom, the letter box labeled "Janet Goleman" was empty when I opened it. I had failed to receive the coveted invitation to pledge my desired sorority. I stumbled out of the mailroom, wallowing in self-pity and wandered aimlessly around campus until I found a park bench to sit on and cry. My quiet hysterics did nothing to relieve my sense of rejection and shock. Once I regained some calm, I reviewed the events of my sorority invitation period and tried to fathom the first abject failure of my eighteen years on Earth.

I kept replaying the events of the meetings the sorority sisters conducted to select their future pledges. I thought I'd be a shoo-in because I was so confident in my social and conversational skills, honed from multiple campaigns running for office.

What went wrong?

Was I too pushy?

Maybe too tall or not cute enough?

Did my clothing style fit in?

I created this list of negativities that might possibly explain this rejection and my failure to achieve the sorority "bid" I had dreamed about. But nothing helped. I was heartbroken.

Later that day, my sense of purpose was thankfully recharged by a telephone call from my best friend, Naomi. However, it didn't exactly start out that way.

"Janet," she screamed, "I got it. I got Phi Eps bid to pledge!"

I could barely speak.

"Janet, why are you quiet?"

I could barely breathe.

"Janet, are you still there?"

"Yes," I cried out, sobbing.

"You didn't get your invitation?"

"No."

My cries reached a fever pitch.

"There must be some mistake," Naomi said. "So many sorority sisters loved you. Okay, Janet, don't worry about a thing. I just decided that I'm not accepting Phi Ep's bid. If they don't want you, I don't want them."

"Are you crazy?" I screamed. "Don't you dare give that up! I won't let you."

"My mind is made up, kiddo! We'll handle Penn together without a sorority."

We argued for hours until exhaustion set in, so we reconvened the discussion the next day, when we weren't so emotional. Although I tried to bribe, connive and plead with Naomi to change her mind, it was to no avail.

"Without you," she said, "I can't, and won't, be a sorority sister. That's all there is to it. Discussion over."

Naomi's shocking, joyful and loving revelation set me straight, right then and there. My renewed self-confidence boosted any sense of rejection I felt and quickly lifted me to the heights of emotional recovery and a new path to success.

By the time I graduated from Penn with Honors, I was also President of KDE, the School of Education's Honorary Society, and represented our university at an Education Symposium for students in Chicago. I was also pictured in *The Philadelphia Daily News* for receiving Penn's Hey Day Ceremony's Graduating Senior Service Award.

Looking back at that time, I realize that there were few instances during my seventeen years before entering college when I hadn't achieved my goals. That is not to say I was never reprimanded growing up or never received a smack on my fanny, growing up. But basically, I was the proverbial star girl of the '50s who followed orders to a tee, excelled in scholastic work and won all the elections I entered.

After such a long stretch of success, my greatest disappointment in college became my rallying cry for further achievement as an undergraduate.

There's a song with a powerful message, made famous by Kelly Clarkson many years after I graduated, called, "What Doesn't Kill You, Makes You Stronger." Of course, I wasn't familiar with those lyrics back then, but I surely exemplified those words as I plowed my way through my studies, raking in super grades.

I joined the college newspaper and loved covering events on campus, started my first job selling textbooks at the start of each semester at Zavelle's Book Store and rose through the ranks of Kappa Delta Epsilon, the School of Education Honor Society.

As a senior, I represented my university at the KDE national convention in Chicago and flew there alone on a plane for the first time. At the Women's Government Hey Day Award ceremony, right before graduation, I was honored with the School of Education Award and happily was pictured in *The Philadelphia Daily News*, collecting the prize.

The best outcome of my college sorority crisis was the relationship cemented forever between Naomi and myself. After learning how to lick my emotional wounds and recover from my sorority rejection, she and I spent the next three and a half years, arm in arm, accelerating our course work so we could complete our undergraduate education degrees. Our friendship has flourished throughout all these years and I proudly claim her as a close friend to this very day.

How lucky for me!

By the way, both of us found time to extend our other arm to the two fine young men we would eventually marry after college. In fact, all of my academic success paled in comparison to my proudest accomplishment of my college career.

I became joyfully engaged to my beloved hero, Bert Felgoise.

*Jan's Brushes
with History*

I have always been a history buff.
Maybe that's because I was a toddler
when World War II exploded.
By the time I could spell my name,
I could also pronounce big scary words,
like invasion and patriotic and Japanese,
even though I wasn't totally sure what any of them meant.
As I grew up through this defining experience,
I think I noticed that the world was much bigger
than my own family and neighborhood
and that there was a lot I needed to keep track of
that was affecting our lives.

Jan's Brushes with History

Part 1

Life During WW II
August 7, 1941

I WAS THREE YEARS OLD when the United States was brutally attacked by a Japanese air-raid on Pearl Harbor and entered World War II. Although I was too young to know anything about war, and its ramifications, sacrifices and implications on our country, I knew that being "patriotic" meant I was actively involved in helping the war effort. I had no idea about the purpose of our Victory Garden, but I helped my family grow our own produce in our large backyard. I learned to plant seeds, pull out unruly weeds and harvest vegetables during those five-years.

I also became quite good at stepping on things.

"Janet, this is how you stomp on tin cans," my big brother said, "after the top and bottom is removed, to flatten them out. Then we'll collect them in a box so they can be picked up and used to help the war effort."

"What's a war effort?" I said.

Food shopping with my mother meant carefully calculating our food stamps and rationing coupons, which were also necessary for purchasing gasoline. Our family was fortunate because my father's factory manufactured war supplies, which meant he had a car sticker that enabled him to purchase gasoline so he could drive to work.

"Daddy, am I holding the steering wheel, right?"

I always asked when I sat on his lap behind the circular wheel with my arms outstretched. There were few motor vehicles on the streets because of gas rationing so we had no worries about other cars being too close.

Air raid drills, with their loud, wailing alarms were my favorite. They announced a new practice session to prepare for potential emergencies. That clamoring sound was our signal to scurry throughout our home and lower black window shades over the white ones to prevent any light from showing through. That precaution created a "blackout" against any potential air raid attack by the enemy of America.

"Get ready because Mr. Smedley will be stopping by to check how we did with our blackout shades."

I was fascinated by our Neighborhood Air Raid Warden's uniform, which included a black metal helmet that extended behind his head to cover his neck and meet the collar of his long raincoat.

"I can't wait to touch his black metal hat when he comes to inspect our shades."

What a thrill to meet him when he came to inspect our preparations and give us an A-okay for our performance. How we wished we could try on his hat, too, but he had too many inspections to accommodate our requests!

"Suck 'emmed" to His Illness
April 12, 1945

I WAS ALMOST SEVEN YEARS OLD. It was a Saturday, and I was lying on the living room floor, coloring, in front of the radio console, listening to my favorite afternoon programs. Suddenly, a stern voice interfered with the entertainment.

"We interrupt this program to bring you the tragic news that the President of the United States has succumbed to his illness at 3:35 p.m."

"What's 'suck 'emmed' mean?" I said aloud. "I better ask Mom. It's about the President."

I found her talking to Aunt Reba, our next-door neighbor, on the landing we shared between our two houses.

"Mommy, I just heard on the radio that the President 'suck 'emmed' to his illness."

"What are you talking about?"

"He 'suck 'emmed'" I said. "I don't know."

"Oh my God," Aunt Reba said. "Do you think that she heard the word succumbed?"

"Oh no!" my mother screamed. "He died!"

We all ran into our house where the radio was still presenting details of Franklin D. Roosevelt's death. Aunt Reba and my mother were sobbing and clinging to each other, so there was nothing else for me to do but cry along with 'em.

General Douglas MacArthur Is Fired
April 12, 1951

I RUSHED TO GET TO MY SEAT on time in Mr. Gewertz's history class at Sayre Jr. High. My classmates and I were hysterical. It was the day after President Harry S. Truman relieved our hero, Douglas MacArthur, of his responsibilities as Commander of American forces in Korea. He was fired! How could this have happened to one of the greatest war heroes ever? This was the general who departed from the Philippines after the Japanese attack, with the heroic promise that became as iconic as any quote in our history.

"I shall return?"

We couldn't wait for class to begin so we could discuss this upsetting news. We were all aligned in support for our hero and against the President, who obviously made a big mistake.

How would our country recover from this catastrophe?

Mr. Gewertz, who was a great supporter of class discussion, tried to calm us down with some information we might not have known.

"How many know about the difference in the plans that the General and the President supported and proposed?" he said.

"We know that the General went into North Korea and was beaten back by a wave of Chinese who helped the North Koreans," David said.

"But did you know that he wanted to carry out some atomic bombing?"

That information sent shock waves throughout the class. Mr. Gewertz filled us in on the differences between the famous General and the President's agendas and the importance of atomic containment. That information seemed to level the argument. We all felt so grown up that we could analyze differences of opinion about values for dealing with foreign countries.

When the General returned to the United States and addressed Congress, we cheered when we heard his unforgettable words.

"Old Soldiers never die; they just fade away."

A RIOTOUS ROMP THROUGH MOTHERHOOD

The Great Diaper Deodorizer Drama of 1967

LIFE GOT CHALLENGING FAST, with two baby boys, born fourteen months apart, all while I was in the process of completing my Master's Degree in Education. I get tired just thinking about it.

Ever since I lined up my dolls as a young girl in my make-believe classroom, I wanted to be a teacher. It had nothing to do with the fact that my mother was a teacher before she and my father started their family. I just always enjoyed parading in front of my attentive students, even though they were predictably glassy-eyed, silent and never asked questions. I was fascinated to find out how it be with actual human beings.

After teaching history for six years in the highly rated Cheltenham School District, I retired from the classroom to welcome our first baby. I still needed a few more courses to complete my credentialing. I was surprised when another pregnancy "appeared out of nowhere," and since our second child was due to arrive soon, I limited my Temple University graduate school classes to once a week on Saturdays.

A few months later, thanks to the care of a most reliable babysitter, I was able to leave my babies for hours at a time and complete my course work in March of 1967, when Marc, our oldest, was 22 months.

One day, as I was about to leave the apartment for a morning of classes, I reminded Patsy about something significant in Marc's ongoing development.

"Don't forget to check out the diaper pail lid," I said.

With that invaluable bit of advice, I left.

Marc had re4cently developed a keen interest in the green colored, stiff, crinkly sounding cellophane paper, which was used to envelope the diaper-pail deodorant. He was fascinated with the unique sounds, which emanated as I unwrapped each new circular disc, as I replaced the used one. He also liked to inhale the sweet odors from the diaper bucket.

When I returned home four hours later, I opened the front door and yodeled cheerfully, as I usually did.

"Everything fine?"

I placed my keys on the table and greeted Patsy, who looked perfectly calm, as if nothing unusual was going on.

"We had a great time at lunch," she said. "Roy should be getting up from his nap soon."

Across the room, Marc was totally absorbed in a new puzzle. When he looked up to exclaim, "Hiya, Mommy!" I was dumbstruck. His wide smile was illuminated with shiny glimmers of light, sparkling all around his mouth.

"Oh, my God! The diaper deodorizer!"

I ran into the boys' bedroom. Right next to the changing table, I saw the diaper pail lid on the floor and the deodorizer missing from its' hole. With all the noise I was making, Roy woke up crying from his nap. Marc quickly added to the chaos, as he ran into the bedroom, lights flashing from his mouth, to find out why I was screaming. Patsy tended to Roy as I grabbed Marc and raced to the bathroom to find the bottle of Ipekak, a vomit-inducing drug, which was a staple of every household in those days with young children. Once I gave Marc a full dose, I bundled him up, grabbed some towels for mopping-up, along with a pot from under the stove, and raced out of the apartment for my car, clutching my son and all the paraphernalia hanging off of both of us.

Marc next to me on the front seat, fortified with towels and the metal pot, as I sped off for Abington Hospital. What a bizarre couple we must have been for the other cars we passed. I was singing songs at the top of my lungs, trying to distract Marc with his favorite song.

"Yankee Doodle went to town, a-riding on his pony . . ."

Marc, who sat stiff and motionless with towels stuffed around him, brandishing a cooking utensil between his legs, stared at me incredulously.

If Woody Allen had driven by, he would have started the cameras rolling to catch this nutty scene. Imagine a hysterical mother driving like a lunatic with her little son who like his mouth belonged in a science fiction movie.

As we whisked through the revolving door of the emergency room, I screamed.

"Help! My son just ate the diaper deodorizer!"

It was as if the staff knew I was coming. Two nurses ran over and yanked Marc from my arms as the metal pot I was holding crashed to the floor, adding to what was already an unusually noisy ER. Marc and the nurses vanished quickly without inviting me to enter through the slowly closing doors of the examination room.

I collapsed into a wheelchair, the only unoccupied seat in the packed waiting room, exasperated, trying to catch my breath before seeking a payphone to contact my husband, the father of this luminous little creature we called our son.

Waiting by myself among a room of strangers was traumatic. Every time I began to moan about my situation, I stopped, imagining what my little boy was going through, and all by himself!

I was soon advised that he had to have his stomach pumped because of the poisonous deodorizer he had partially ingested, as he hadn't regurgitated nearly enough from the over-the-counter medicine I had administered.

The wait felt endless, as I grew more and more worried and agitated. Finally, after what seemed like a minute short of forever, my demeanor instantly changed dramatically as Marc appeared, comfortable in the arms of a nurse, smiling that famous smile of his!

Just at that moment, Bert entered the ER and the three of us enjoyed a noisy, delirious hug, jumping up and down to the tune of, you guessed it, "Yankee Doodle." With my heart firmly positioned back in my chest, I held Marc tight as we headed to the parking lot.

"I'll have to do a better job training your taste buds, little guy," Bert said, kissing his son and winking at me.

At that moment, I was too emotionally exhausted to even smile, but it was a cute joke to retell later on, especially with Marc's children.

Boudin and Me

FINALLY! BERT AND I were on our first vacation since Glenn had been born two years earlier in 1970, which completed our progeny of four sons in four and a half years. Our brood was complete and as much as we loved each of our boys, we welcomed the break.

One afternoon, while enjoying the great weather in Palm Beach, Florida, we ended up meandering around inside the famous Wally Findlay Art Gallery. We didn't flinch as we walked right into this prestigious art emporium, known far and wide from the tip of Florida to their Fifth Avenue gallery in Manhattan.

Of course, we had no idea about the artist's legacy of the painting we became attracted to. We were too busy admiring the large, colorful painting of nineteenth century ladies parading along the Normandy Coast of France on a sunny afternoon, wearing full-skirted long dresses. We knew nothing about the custom of afternoon beach promenades, which were so popular at that time. We also had no idea about the artist, Eugene Boudin.

As totally irrational tourists, far away from the normalcy of our typical middle-class environment, we simply had to have this painting! We were drawn to the loose, flowing brush strokes, which created the beach scene and the closer we came to the painting, we recognized how vague the images became. It was like a visual magic trick. The dramatic gold-colored frame with numerous curves carved into it only added to the overall enticement, which led to our unpredictable purchase.

We consummated the sale by using our credit card and literally skipped out of the gallery, feeling so proud at having purchased our first major art investment. We arrived back home in Philadelphia before the painting was delivered and were thrilled when it arrived, encapsulated like a treasure in a large wooden crate.

Once the children were tucked into bed that night, we undid the complicated, protective packaging and unveiled our first masterpiece. We were both enraptured by the grandeur of the painting. That is, before I reviewed the bill of lading, which accompanied our prize.

"Look how great this will look on our living room wall," Bert said.

"It's so large," I said. "I don't remember it looking so wide when we were in the gallery."

"The colors are so bright," he said.

"How come it's so difficult to see the details of their faces?" I said.

Bert shrugged.

"I'm in such a state of shock about the bill, Bert. I can't get over that we really spent five thousand dollars for this artwork. Now that we're home from vacation, I'm beginning to think more rationally."

"What do you mean, rationally?"

"Five thousand dollars is a fortune! Were we a little high?"

Bert laughed.

"We loved this painting so much in the gallery! What's the matter? Now, all you're gasping about is the money!"

"I can't believe we spent all this money for a painting! It's so wildly expensive. Do you realize we bought our house six years ago and this painting costs one-seventh the cost of our entire home? I can't fathom how we spent this much money."

"Stay calm, relax, we'll talk about it tomorrow after we've had a night to sleep on it." My buyer's remorse was roaring in my ears, so much so that I never slept at all that night. Ultimately our beautiful, very large Boudin oil painting was shipped back to the gallery and the refund check was promptly sent to us. I was so relieved, at least at the time.

After this original Findlay Gallery purchase, as irrational as it may have been, I became immersed in art appreciation.

Early on, I started an Art Goes to School group of volunteers in my local Lower Moreland School District. After taking classes at The Philadelphia Museum of Art, we presented reproductions of a set of paintings to local elementary school classes.

This was the preparatory groundwork that my four sons had to endure as their mother entered into their elementary school classrooms. Little did they know, it was much better than the more dramatic times they endured when they got to high school and discovered me as their substitute teacher!

Soon, I worked my way through the ranks of Art Goes to School to become President of the 23 local chapters in the Delaware Valley. My study of art history flourished during this period, as well as the growth of our art collection.

Forty-six years after this first excursion into the art collectors' world, in April 2018, I spent six days on a study tour at The Art institute of Chicago. The famous museum boasts a grand exhibition hall of Impressionist paintings.

I immediately re-connected with Eugene Boudin.

The difference between now and then was that now, I knew all about his place in art history. Boudin was a nineteenth century artist who discovered what's known as painting "en pleine air."

He was captivated by painting outdoors with his oil paints, brushes and easel, capturing the magic of the shimmering effects of the sun, transforming colors of the ocean, beaches and people's clothing.

He had a great influence on Monet, the more famous of the two Impressionists, who left the Normandy Coast to Paris to live and study in Paris. Boudin enticed the younger Monet to return to his hometown to study with him. There, they discovered the effect sunlight had on their subjects as they painted outdoor scenes instead of painting inside of their ateliers, as was so common at the time.

Luckily for the art world, Monet obeyed his mentor and returned to his birthplace to learn how to enhance his painting skills with the effects of outdoor sunlight. The rest is history; that is Monet's place in the world of Impressionism. Although Boudin never migrated to Paris, nor achieved the fame of the Impressionist Masters, his works are featured in museums around the world. Today, he is remembered as being an early proponent of Impressionism.

When I returned home from my Art Institute of Chicago study tour, I started to investigate current auction prices for Boudin's work. A 2018 sale at Sotheby's in New York of a small painting of his fetched $1.3 million dollars. Not a bad return on a five-thousand-dollar investment after forty plus years, wouldn't you agree? Sadly, I lost all bragging rights about art history or enhanced investments on the day we returned our Boudin painting to the art gallery in Florida, more than forty years ago.

"She Who Must Be Obeyed"

ONE SUMMER, WHEN THE BOYS were growing up fast, we encountered an unexpected learning curve for all of us. My dear friends, Elaine and Phil Cohen, were co-presidents of the Philadelphia chapter of Children's International Summer Villages. One of their sons was participating in a six-week summer exchange program, which had organized ten students from our area to host ten students from Sweden.

"Sure, Elaine," I said one hot afternoon, "bring the Swedish CISV group over to use our pool for a swim."

That invitation jettisoned my four sons into a European adventure they had never anticipated or dreamed about. As this gang of twenty teens cavorted wildly in our pool, my four sons literally hid inside our house, completely uninterested in having anything to do with the backyard frivolity. They held their position for the duration of the program.

Undeterred by their lack of interest, I convinced Marc, my oldest, to sign up for the exchange program the following summer. He was raring to go, excited to welcome our new Finnish guest, Kalle.

Because we had recently lost the head of our family, the exchange program was a great diversion for all of us. Kalle, who became the fifth boy in our home, provided lots of fun and kept us laughing about his sauna customs back home.

"You mean you just sit in a small room attached to your house," said Marc, "with steam bubbling all around you, and call that fun?"

"Yeah, it feels really good on your body," said Kalle.

"You keep sitting with other people," I said, "sweating up a storm?"

"We're all family and friends."

The anguished look on my sons' faces gave away their new opinions about saunas.

Besides the fact that I mispronounced his name the entire summer by calling him "Kallay" instead of "Kolleh," we quickly acclimated to his cool and calm demeanor and his delight in being in our home. Kalle even participated frequently as a posse member to recapture our runaway dog, Rex, and he loved swimming in our pool.

The following summer, Roy, my second oldest son, fitfully agreed, both literally and figuratively, to participate in the CISV Exchange. Of course, he had no idea that he didn't have any option, once "She Who Must Be Obeyed" had made up her mind that it was time for him to embark on his first great adventure in life.

First, we had to endure a full-blown temper tantrum, when Roy kicked, screamed and even banged his feet as he spread himself out flat on the den rug and wailed away.

"I'm not going!"

He finally departed for Sweden to visit Thommy, his teammate, albeit less than enthusiastically. Much to his own surprise, I think, his first phone call home revealed his newfound joy.

"Mom, you didn't tell me some Swedish ladies go topless!"

My son's vacation was made in the shade.

The next summer, we had two overlapping visitors for a short time when Marc and Roy hosted their Japanese and Swedish guests. The CISV highlight event was a weekend overnight camping trip with the visiting groups and their American hosts. What could go wrong?

At two a.m. that Sunday night, I received a shocking telephone call.

"Mrs. Felgoise, everyone is safe, but we've had a disturbance at our overnight camp."

"What happened? Are my sons okay?"

"Your sons are safely incommunicado, after having been apprehended in the girls' camp while trying to meet up with some of the female campers—unannounced *and* uninvited."

I didn't know whether to laugh or cry.

"Mrs. Felgoise, I'm sorry, but you will have to be here early tomorrow morning to remove your boys from the camp."

As I was serving at the time as the vice-president of the CISV Philadelphia chapter, ready to assume the presidency that fall, my embarrassment at this revelation knew no bounds!

As I drove to the camp site the next morning, I envisioned myself being cool, calm and composed, no matter what.

"Don't say a word," I hissed. "Just get into the car."

My lips were tight, my spine was straight, and my fists were almost clenched into two humiliated little balls as the villains were marched out to be discharged.

"Gentlemen," I said, doing my best imitation of Golda Meir, "your punishment for sullying the Felgoise reputation is stopping with me as I stop to investigate every single antique shop along the way home"

"No, please! Not that torture!"

I had anticipated their cries of psychological pain as they knew what they would suffer through for the duration of the two-hour trip back home. Obviously, this little cultural tour was the perfect punishment for boys being boys.

Brian, 16-years-old by then, participated in an exchange a year later. His mate was also a Finnish lad, who lived way north from Kalle's home in Helsinki. One of the highlights of Brian's exchange was a short trip to St. Petersburg, Russia.

"Mom, you have to visit The Hermitage Art Museum," he said, raving about the experience. "The paintings are awesome."

At first, hearing this news, I couldn't believe Brian was actually my son.

It reminded me of when I had once resorted to "hog tying" all four boys and dragging them to The Philadelphia Museum of Art to see what I thought would grab them with wild abandon. Oh my God, was I wrong. Landseer's fabulous exhibition, which drew flocks of breathless visitors to view his paintings of unique wild animals, was wasted on the Felgoise Four. Now, hearing Brian rave about seeing paintings in one of the greatest collections in the world, I was eternally grateful to CISV for his about-faced appreciation of fine art.

Glenn, on the other hand, was lucky to once again escape experiencing the travails of his three older brothers. First, by the time he arrived at Lower Moreland High School, he was saved from one of their most harrowing experiences. He avoided all the embarrassment that they had to handle when walking into a classroom to find the substitute for the day.

"Hey, Felgoise, you better behave, because your mom is our sub this period."

"Oh, no," was the usual painful retort.

Although my sons may have suffered when I was their substitute, I was the happiest one the school had ever seen. Usually, such teachers are "eaten for breakfast" by the students they temporarily supervise. But I was special because I had the follow-up protection of the Felgoise boys, which meant nobody caused me any problems in my classes. But at the dinner table in the evening, it was a different story. By then, my teaching joy had vanished.

"Mom, why did you have to ruin my day, and make that joke? You were the only one who laughed!"

"Really, Mom? You embarrassed me *again*!"

"Could you just change your last name or something next time?"

Glenn avoided the painful "child of the substitute" experience because by then I was fully invested as a student in Temple Law School and was no longer available to work as a sub. He was also rescued from having to participate in a CISV exchange to Costa Rica, as the country was under siege by revolutionary forces.

However, he eventually became the winner of a grand touring experience. As a college student, he participated in Semester at Sea, sailing around the world with 600 other collegians for fifteen weeks, receiving credits for courses he took aboard ship. His experience was the ultimate one out of all the boys because he discovered and planned this amazing excursion without any initiative from his mother.

My influence in my children's lives, as "She Who Must Be Obeyed," wasn't limited to their summer exploits. I also had a hand in engineering my sons' musical experience when they entered Lower Moreland High School. Marc joined the high school's unique sport of water polo when he became a freshman and the other three boys went out for the football team.

Boys. Sports. Okay. Until I laid down the law.

"If you want to participate in a high school sport of any kind, fine, but you must play an instrument in the school band."

I was probably inspired by reading a fairy tale about brothers forming a band and working their way through college. Even though that scenario differed from ours, as all of those brothers attended the same college, that idea generated my sons' great challenge.

The younger three had all been participated in community football, so the ground rules were a foregone conclusion. There would be no joining the marching band, as that would conflict with the weekly football games, so that left participation in the concert band.

"The only benefit about being in the band, Mom, is that we don't have to lug our instruments home after every practice."

"Yeah," said Roy, "three of us practice in band one period a day, so we leave our stuff in the band room."

I was such a lucky mother because I had no rebellious men in my family. I believed that they all participated in the band for four straight years, or so I thought. Many years later, I was advised, when they confessed, that Brian didn't play anything at all! After his second year, when his older brothers graduated, he dropped out. Glenn never even started when he arrived at the high school.

Going to law school had really compromised my diligence and sidetracked my attention to details, such as musical instruments and the occasional concert. I was so absorbed in my own studies that I didn't have time to notice my own sons pulling one over on me. Nevertheless, the two "cop-outs" continued on with their football careers, minus the musical notes to accompany their actions.

Through no fault of the L.M. High School Band, Marc won a four-year water polo scholarship to the University of Richmond. Roy won a four-year scholarship to play football at Hofstra University, and Brian won a year at the U.S. Naval Academy Prep School for his prowess as a quarterback.

As their proud mother, I marched along each day to my own tune, thinking that I was the one being obeyed.

By the way, the title of this essay comes from the BBC series *Rumpole of the Bailey*, which is about a barrister who solves crimes and is well respected as an English advocate, even as he cowers in deference to his wife. Although he never names her, he refers to her as "she who must be obeyed."

I think it makes a provocative (and telling) title for this story.

How I Became Famous as a Mother of Four Sons

BERT AND I WAITED SIX YEARS after we got married, while he finished law school and started a legal practice, before we demonstrated our talents in the baby boom business. Four years and nine months later, I was the frantic, overwhelmed, exhausted mother of a gaggle of four bouncing boys.

Luckily, those were the days when babysitters cost only fifty cents an hour, so I was able to relax sometimes and enjoy the domestic riot at home. My other secret weapon for family management was having a built-in playgroup of brothers, always ready for diversion, fun and playtime. I kept at least one boy available to play with one or two or three of the others at all times, a formula that saved me more times than I can count.

Our homegrown, built-in team was the key to my survival and success. Those boys provided all the distraction necessary—for each other—right at home by keeping each other busy with self-created activities.

Eenie, Meenie, Miney, Moe . . .

That summed up my distinction as the proud possessor of four sons!

Sometimes, it was like watching a bunch of puppies chasing their own tails. I felt so comfortable managing these four early on that I supported our adoption of a fifth boy, a dog named Rex. I figured he can't talk back and what's one more mouth to feed?

As the team got older, their job charts replaced the constant fun and games and our household turned into a well-oiled machine, a virtual tool factory with its division of departmentalized labor. Depending on age and talents, we worked out the labor pool categories.

Of course, it helped that our oldest son slipped easily into the commanding role of family "concierge." At that time, I wasn't even familiar with that word or its loaded history. As the "capo," Marc naturally evolved into the top dog who barked orders to the rest of the pack. What Bert and I didn't bargain for was that we would also be saluting our son as he began to run the house quite proficiently! He determined the daily regimen to maintain the orderly process of management and we all acquiesced to his practical plans.

It wasn't long before our family gained some celebrity status throughout the neighborhood and through the boys' school and sports activities. There was just one other gaggle of four sons in our town, but they were older and more diverse in age than our team.

Three blond heads and one dark-haired adorable guy always seemed to elicit the same reactions from passers-by.

"Is that kid with the dark hair, yours, too?"

"Sure is," I always said, as Brian was quick to pout.

He made up for being the dark-haired bunny, genetically connected to me, by becoming the star athlete of our group. He created this role of the gladiator through his prowess, strength and agility on the playing fields of Lower Moreland Township.

Roy had the distinction of becoming the Casanova of the clan. His laid-back manner and handsome looks sent out silent vibrations to the ladies, who constantly congregated around him. His "aw shucks" demeanor and nonchalance just encouraged the damsels, like flies soaring blindly into flypaper. He seemed to operate below the radar and piled up friends, many of whom just happened to be gals.

Glenn, the youngest, naturally developed a great sense of patience as he always got a bit of extra attention being the last kid to learn new tricks from his three older siblings. Happiest and most content to pick up the slack at the end of the line, he gained the distinction of handing me my greatest surprise of motherhood.

As I was coasting along, enjoying my fame as one of the progenitors of four healthy, well-adjusted, clean-cut kids, one fateful day put a shocking crimp in my normally smooth style.

Glenn, most unexpectedly out of all four of my boys, was arrested!

He had lived a crime-free life for fifteen years until the day he was rounded up by the township police for ringing neighbors' doorbells and jumping into a waiting car to escape.

Normal parental embarrassment could not begin to camouflage my feelings as I flew to the jail (in a car) to collect him. The police let him go without any fanfare, but Glenn faced a more daunting imprisonment at home, locked up in his own bedroom for a prolonged period of penitence. Hopefully, he's learned his lesson by now.

All in all, our community loved my sons. The Felgoise Boise ran as a posse through the neighborhood each time the "Rex alarm" bell sounded. Whenever that occurred, neighboring doors flew open en masse as their friends joined the search and rescue operation to return the hunter dog who had escaped (again) from our home.

I have photographs showing groups of searchers heading home with our black and white Springer Spaniel in tow, looking proud of accomplishing his capture. These missions were a collaborative effort latest and each roundup notched another success on the team's belts, with the help of many friends and passers-by. Each time I witnessed the neighborhood coming together, with my boys at the helm, I felt so satisfied to be their mother.

Did I have a great deal to feel proud of, co-parenting these wonderful guys? You Bet!

Were these four young men, who adjusted so bravely to the untimely death of their father, brave and courageous? You Bet!

Did I enjoy my fame in the community as the mother of a fearless foursome, who all became such standouts as young men? You Bet!

Too Busy to "Mother"

I WAS ONE FRANTICALLY BUSY LADY in 1982, trying to ride herd over four teenaged boys, ages 12 to 16, while remaining quite involved in community affairs.

In addition to serving on the Huntingdon Valley Library Board, substitute teaching at Lower Moreland High School, and participating on the 22 Delaware Valley Community Art Goes to School Board, an art enrichment program for elementary school students, I had to squeeze in a dedicated day to work at a non-profit, the Childtowne Montessori Nursery School.

I founded this special educational center with four friends in the early '70s so that my children could enjoy Maria Montessori's unique learning environment. Each of the two classrooms consisted of children aged three to five, who pursued independent activities after receiving instruction from their teachers. By age five, children at our school were working with blocks and counting arithmetic concepts in the hundreds and thousands, as well as reading stories phonetically.

I was delighted to fulfill my cultural aspirations and leadership roles while the boys spent their days in school.

When our family tragedy occurred on April 27, 1982, our lives changed dramatically. When the leader of our family died that night, I instantly became smothered in grief and what seemed like a never-ending web of legal entanglements related to closing Bert's law practice. On top of that was a larger drama involving the resolution of a $12 million construction loan for Pine Woods Development, the housing project he had created, which had ceased production due to a 22 percent interest rate at the time. My support team of lawyers, accountants and relatives attempted to sell the construction company and preserve the ownership of our Huntingdon Valley home, which was included in the construction loan.

Of course, all of this put a hold on my volunteer activities so I could dig my way out of these financial obligations. I must admit that Marc's management skills kept our family together more that my parenting as I was completely overwhelmed with negotiations to resolve the Pine Woods financial settlement.

At the end of each weekday, I was exhausted by the time all four boys returned home at six for dinner, following their respective sports programs.

Marc was the water polo goalie, a unique sport in all area high schools at the time and Roy, Brian and Glenn worked out on the football field. We gathered for dinner and created plans for survival tactics.

My feeble dinner attempts were reduced to popping TV dinners into the microwave. The boys assumed their roles, based on a rotating job chart with designated duties for the upkeep of our pool and an acre of land.

We relaxed together on weekends while trying to adjust to missing a parent and a husband. I often marveled at how the boys grew so tall in spite of the food desert I provided.

Finally, a resolution to the Pine Woods Construction Company was secured in 1983, and our house was salvaged from the bank's oppression. A home builder purchased one property at a time from the project, as interest rates decreased, and we were home free. My big commercial business lesson was that no one purchases for retail what can be obtained at a fire sale.

Amidst all the depressing, exhaustive and frightening moments in the legal construction resolution, a positive emerged from being involved with the legal ramifications that monopolized my life during this time.

I became intrigued by the power of knowledge about the law as it applied to our financial problems. It was hard to believe that I wasn't remotely interested when Bert went through law school or even shared legal remedies with me when he began his practice.

Now, I was paying obsessively close attention to suggested legal strategies offered by my team and was caught up in the resolution of my personal financial drama about how my family would survive, if at all.

1982 and 1983 were a blur when it came to the daily responsibilities of being a mother. I'm not sure how I managed it all, but somehow, I did, thanks to the love and support of my four hungry boys.

Shut the Door

When you let self-pity slip all over you
And allow regret to slither and wrap all around,
It's time to shake out that serpent view
That holds you down and forces you aground.

Free up from that crawling impediment
That sneaks up silently out of nowhere,
By facing it boldly with resentment
To dare threaten your peace with despair.

Stand strong to banish negative power
And extinguish false flames of remorse,
For all hurts and memories that sour
Your usual happier, well-adjusted course.

Life brings its own challenges to ponder
Just how we can carry out each day
Let alone voluntarily falling asunder
And allow defeatist thoughts to hold sway.

Shut the Door on any negativity
That creeps up on you from down below.
This mantra will work well to set you free
From the pain and doubt you'll no longer know.

The Journey to My Legal Career

WHERE DID I EVER GET THE UNMITIGATED gumption to decide to go to law school?

I certainly wasn't a shrinking violet. While successfully running a Montessori nursery school with four others, I became president of the 26 chapters of Art Goes to School of Delaware Valley and led a group of 22 independent women on a London Art Tour.

I didn't flinch when I had a chance to break into a new career of public relations. After having promoted a successful Merchants' Week in Huntingdon Valley to support our library, I snagged a trial run at Boefinger & Associates PR firm. I was hoping to wow them over with my talents to allow me to continue working part-time, while raising our four boys.

Quite unexpectedly, I was felled by an internal infection, which required abdominal surgery, and that ended my short-lived career in public relations. I navigated those challenges in addition to starting a Brandeis reading group in my community and wrote a weekly column in the local *Breeze* newspaper.

But law school? Was I meschugeneh?

After the sudden death of my husband in 1982, I was thrust into a legal arena of dealing with a hungry bank that required the repayment of a multi-million-dollar construction loan for a housing project undertaken by Bert, with our homestead as collateral. I also had to manage closing down his law practice after his associate absconded with many client files.

As I review these events, I can pinpoint the exact moment when I became "Jan of Arc" and announced that I was going to become an attorney to "protect my family." The turning point to one of the most significant decisions of my life came from a comment made to me by the leading senior attorney handling our case. When I confessed to him that I was seriously interested in becoming involved with the law, his comment took me by surprise as he leaned across his desk to pat my hand and encourage me.

"Why don't you become a paralegal?" he said.

Really? Did he just say that to me?

The gauntlet was thrown down. It was decided. I was going to law school!

In that moment, I saw my future blazing before me. The essence of what it would take to become a lawyer was pulsating inside me and I was raring to go, age and gender be dammed.

That lawyer's patronizing tone and sarcastic encouragement only made me more convinced that I was going to set out on a plan I had never dreamed about. That impetus, born from my anger at his condescending attitude, plus supportive encouragement from two attorney friends, drove me to meet the challenge of my life. Up until that time, the most exotic, dramatic thing I had done had been traveling abroad on my own the summer before I entered law school.

The courage it took for me to go halfway across the world to a land where I couldn't speak a word of their native language sparked my courage for taking on an even bigger adventure. Breaking into study mode after a fifteen-year hiatus since completing my Masters' program would be a much bigger mountain to climb, but I was up for it.

Before I could start in as a full-time student, my first task was disengaging from all the activities I was involved in as a community leader in my Lower Moreland Township community.

I retired from the board of directors of the Montessori school, which four friends and I had founded twelve years earlier in a rented church building. Although we hired specially trained teachers, we each assumed a supervisory position one day a week and now I had to give that up. The school had earned a stellar reputation in our community and Lower Bucks County.

I also departed my position as vice-president of the Huntingdon Valley Library Board of Directors where I'd served many years, mostly fund raising through special events. I was most proud of my Merchants' Week Extravaganza, which touted all the businesses in our town of Huntingdon Valley with give-away coupon gifts for community supporters.

All four boys cheered my decision to retire from the library because it meant they wouldn't have to do volunteer duty as models aboard the Fourth of July float, which the library sponsored each year. They were also quite happy about me no longer subbing at their school, despite the fact that we had worked out an intricate plan of non-engagement, where they would each sit in the back of their respective classrooms and hide.

"Mom, did you have to make that ridiculous comment when Steve asked a question?"

"Who's Steve?"

That was typical of our banter back at home, but from then on, that would be over, too. My days as the "Goises" mom were done and no substitute, before or after, was ever afforded such respect and cooperation as I received; I am sure of that.

"Be cool" was the message telegraphed throughout Lower Moreland High, whenever I appeared, and I would miss that.

My plan to become a law student rescued Marc, Roy and Brian from further embarrassment—at last. They always congratulated Glenn from escaping these hardships because he was in Middle School at the time and didn't have to suffer when he arrived at the high school, because I was gone.

Lastly, I turned in my byline at the *Breeze*, our local paper, where I covered a few communities in our Montgomery County region. My "In the Valley" column was retired after many years of reporting about local activities, such as school musicals, community sports league specials and every Boy Scott and Girl Scout event around town. I had been kept busy for years on the telephone, responding to publicity efforts of clubs in the area to provide news. As much as I enjoyed doing that, I was also sometimes overwhelmed by the pressure of getting my current weekly article printed by the prescribed deadline, so I was not terribly unhappy to leave my carved out, niche column behind for the expanded reading materials law school would entail.

Erasing the cobwebs darkening my brain synapses while parenting a college freshman, a high school senior and a sophomore, plus an eighth grader, all in the context of a new solo parental role, was going to be a daunting task, for sure.

This was compounded by my immediate devotion to preparation for LSAT exam testing, law school admissions and the application process. Once again, I was consumed with a great challenge.

We were all in school during the day. I compartmentalized evening study time with the three boys at home, which made for a tight schedule. They seemed proud and boasted that their mom was studying as many hours as they were! If they only knew what I kept doing once they went to sleep!

Escape to Japan

BEFORE EMBARKING ON MY UNIVERSITY studies and a new career, I had a journey planned to visit my oldest son's exchange student in Japan. Takatashi had spent the summer with us the year before and we made arrangements for me to visit his family the following summer, which had now arrived. As a long-time collector of oriental artifacts and art, I was looking forward to this trip as an escape from the pressure cooker of legal intrigue I had endured since Bert died. It would be a grand adventure to live with my Japanese son's family in Nagoya for three weeks. Little did I imagine the challenge I would face there, living with the Inukai family, where only Takatashi spoke English.

But wait. I couldn't leave my Fab Four alone. No way. Enter my dear mother, whose compassion for me outweighed her common sense about committing to babysit four teenage grandsons, aged 13 to 18, for three straight weeks.

"Mom, here's a chance of a lifetime!" I said, gushing with excitement. "The Inukai family invited me to come to Nagoya for a visit in appreciation for hosting their son last summer. This is a golden opportunity to renew my batteries after all the legal traumas of settling Bert's estate this year, along with his law practice and the construction business. If you agree to stay here with the boys, I can race off and fly away to Japan."

My mother agreed without hesitation and "hired" to ride herd on the Felgoise boys in my absence. It had always been a daunting task for me to keep up with the summer activities of four young men, so I was concerned about how it would be for a lady thirty years older than me. The boys assured me it would be fine. They were thrilled to escape my compelling presence and considered it a vacation from me without leaving the comfort of their own home.

I fortified my mother with carefully spelled out, written instructions regarding their day camp routines, household chores, allowances, newspaper delivery schedules, and support telephone numbers to call, just in case. Creating this book of directions to cover every possible situation that might arise took so much effort that little time was left for my own preparations.

I had planned to prepare 3x5 index cards with English transliteration of Japanese salutations. This was in addition to a customized cheat-sheet so I could study up on Japanese history and culture before departing on my great adventure. This became another case of the "best laid plans," as I simply had not time to prepare as I wanted.

My brother, Joel, an avid collector of wood block prints by Japanese master artists, called a week before I left, further crowding my prep schedule.

"Jan, while you're in Japan, I'd like you to do me a favor and try to sell some of my prints. I'm hoping you can make a connection through your hosts to sell a small portfolio that you'll take with you. There is a good market in Japan right now, as investors and dealers there want to reclaim some of the fine examples that found their way to America. Will you do it?"

This would have been like bringing coal to Newcastle; not the one in Delaware, the one near London. Although less than enthusiastic about engaging in this deal to bring coals to Newcastle, I couldn't refuse his request.

"Of course, Joel, how can I say no? I'll be your art dealer on my trip because you have been one of my strongest supporters this last year since Bert's death. Besides, your expertise about the Japanese market is a given. I know how much you value the Hiroshige and Hokusai prints you're asking me to try and sell. But since I'm frantically completing a long list of tasks before my departure, there's no time to squeeze in your tutorials on woodblock prints."

I promised to carefully guard his pricey portfolio, hugged my mother and the boys and dashed off to the airport, on my way to a dream trip to Japan.

Takashi, my 18-year-old adopted Japanese son, whom we had dubbed Tash during his visit to our home, welcomed me at the Nagoya airport with his parents.

They whisked me to their beautiful home whose property had been in the family for many generations. I couldn't have imagined such a sprawling, palatial home.

This majestic edifice was incongruously sandwiched between two modest, small homes, more like bungalows, which I had rarely seen in our communities back home, where housing in the same price range are normally clustered together.

Tash's parents were welcoming and gracious and while we didn't understand each other's language, their physical outreach to me was so sincere. We developed a nuanced sign language communication system, aided by Tash, the only one who commanded both languages.

I initially worried about Tosh's grandparents, who had been forced to flee to the mountains to escape American bombers during the war, and if they would welcome me. My worries were exaggerated, as they brought me gifts when they visited.

I quickly learned to be careful when visiting family friends and neighbors with my hosts. The first time I complimented a picture hanging on the wall of their friend's house, it was promptly taken down and presented to me as a gift.

"Tash, please tell Mrs. Suzuki that I think the scroll with flying swallows, hanging over her sofa, is so lovely."

"Mama, Jan, she says thank you and is now taking it down from the wall to give you."

"What? I can't accept such a gift," I said.

"You must accept her generosity because she is your hostess," Tash said.

As soon as I learned about this Japanese tradition, I kept a lid on any further compliments during my frequent visits to the homes of other Japanese visitors who had come to the U.S. with Tash last year.

One day, I joined two of Mrs. Inukai's girlfriends for lunch without Tosh by my side, translating every word. They didn't speak a word of English, and I certainly couldn't speak any Japanese, other than the expressions on my cards. Despite the heavy odds against us, we had a good time conveying information and ideas to each other through sign language and pantomime.

I learned many new customs while visiting the Inukai's relatives and friends. I became efficient when removing my shoes at each entry, neatly stacking them alongside those of the other visitors. I quickly adapted to washing my hands in the sink, which was constructed as a part of the toilet tank and marveled at the efficient use of water from this toilet reservoir.

My hosts generously arranged for hotel accommodations and a guide to meet me after a train ride to Kyoto, the ancient Imperial Capital and religious center of Japan for eleven centuries, which has come to be known all over the world.

There I was, touring and exploring this magical city, all by myself, except for a tour guide. This was an amazing inspirational experience that proved I could do anything I set my mind to do. Taking this cue, I innocently surmised that law school couldn't be any more challenging.

I was overwhelmed by my guide's information.

"There are over 2,000 temples in our city," he said, "in addition to the Palace to compete for tourists' attention."

"Wasn't there any damage almost forty years ago, during the war?" I said.

"Fortunately for our cultural heritage, Kyoto was spared from any atomic bombs during World War II, because of its monumental fame. Because of that decision by the American forces, it became the best-preserved city in Japan."

The architectural variety of pagoda shaped shrines, temples and palaces throughout this city created a great diversity of sights. Just when I thought I had seen all the shapes I could see, I pinched myself when I saw yet another one even more magnificent than the last. I had no idea how rich this city was in its cultural heritage.

Back in Nagoya, Japan's fourth-largest city, Mr. Inukai tried repeatedly to make connections to introduce my brother's portfolio to prospective buyers, but he had no luck. It seemed that art collectors weren't plentiful at all in this largely industrial city. Tokyo was the city I needed to visit in order to peddle these famous, original woodblock prints.

My most exciting Japanese adventure came next, as I traveled on the legendary bullet train from Nagoya to Tokyo for a special meeting. Being on this flying train was thrilling, but it was even better to reconnect with another Japanese visitor who had been in our home the previous year. I was met at the enormous train station with a sign held by Yukie, my teenage chorus visitor and her father. She was part of a school chorus which had performed their way across America. Our family hosted her for a few nights during their concert tour. They returned this hospitality by escorting me around Tokyo for two days. They also presented me with a beautiful sculptured silver and cultured pearl pin. Of all the special places in Tokyo they took me, the beauty and majesty of the Imperial Palace and its gardens won my top prize, hands down, as the most extraordinary sight I saw.

When I returned from Tokyo, the Inukai family entertained me until it was time to board the plane for my return trip home. I still had Joel's portfolio, with the same number of prints, along with a new vertical duffle bag. Although I hadn't been successful selling his art to the Japanese market, that same market did very well in selling to me. Stuffed to the top of the duffle, among my many new treasures of Japanese objects d'art, were the many presents I purchased for my mother and sons, which caused ungainly bulges in my bag.

Our house erupted with joyous noise the minute I opened the front door on my arrival home. Rex, our springer spaniel, howled louder than I had ever heard him yelp. The boys roared their hellos before racing to unscramble the wrapped gifts. They traded them back and forth, desperate to find the one they liked the best.

Unfortunately, my selections didn't make the hit list I had thought they would. The kids made no historical or cultural connections with the exotic Japanese helmets and decorative swords I had selected for them.

The happiest person was Grandmom, because she could finally surrender parental responsibilities, which she had faithfully fulfilled, back to me.

"Jan, here's my report," she said, not wasting any time. "I'm not overworked, underpaid, exhausted or even worn out because the boys took good care of me by doing their jobs to help run the house. Rex ran away only twice and was picked up and returned by the Animal Rescue Patrol. The alarm system went off one time at three in the morning and the police came to check us out. Brian was the only one to suffer a broken bone, just an ankle, at day camp; and I gained five pounds because the cook you hired fed us gourmet meals and the housekeeper kept us on our toes."

"That sounds great," I said. "Thank you, Mother!"

"Guess what?" she said. "If you asked me again to stay with the kids, I'd jump at the chance to be so well taken care of by my grandsons!"

I hugged her tight, as I was so overwhelmed by her comments.

"Be careful what you wish for, Mom. I love you!"

Poor Joel had the opposite reaction, one of great disappointment at my homecoming.

"I can't believe, Jan; not one sale was made. Japanese dealers are bidding all the time at New York art auction houses for these prints and here they were, right under their noses!"

We tried to rationalize the failure of the prints to get any attention and concluded that if I had been in Tokyo, there would have been sales. Licking his wounds, Joel was nevertheless appreciative of my efforts, especially my carrying his portfolio on and off each flight.

I thought back to the long trip, when I had many hours to contemplate the independent experience I had embarked upon as a single traveler to the other side of the world. I had to admit that I was impressed. This trip, originally calculated as an escape from the pressure box I had been locked in, strengthened my resolve and confidence to face the supreme challenge awaiting me at law school.

I felt cleansed from the fear, pain and worry that I had lived through, following the devastation of losing Bert and the complications that ensued. I returned home much stronger in spirit than when I departed. After what I had accomplished, I felt I could handle anything.

Letting Go and Moving On

ALTHOUGH OUR FAMILY TRAGEDY froze our personal outlooks on life for quite some time, a series of important events triggered a process of emotionally opening up to the world again.

Brian's braces miraculously flew off within the year because he stood in front of the mirror every day and commanded his teeth to move. We celebrated Marc's high school graduation in 1983 by hosting 200 of his friends at a class party on our one-acre lot, which was sponsored by a team of graduating neighbors. We also celebrated Glenn's Bar Mitzvah in June and together we trudged through these memorable milestones with collective courage.

My first task upon returning from Japan was getting Marc ready for his freshman year at The University of Richmond. We were all so proud of his four-year scholarship as a water polo player on the school's team. Sponsoring such a unique sport at Lower Moreland High School made it unusual for our geographic area and we were fortunate because one teacher had been an Olympic water polo referee and introduced the sport to our school. Since there were no other high schools participating, the team competed with freshman teams from the Naval Academy, West Point Military Academy, Princeton and other area colleges.

Over time, Marc's team introduced the sport to private high schools in the area, and now, thirty years later, most of the private schools in this part of the state compete in team water polo.

Much to Marc's chagrin, our special delivery team to transport him to college included me, two grandmothers and a special great-aunt. On our ride to Richmond, we stopped at a motel and the five of us emptied our station wagon and even brought Marc's trunk into our room.

Imagine the chaos we created the next day as we crowded into a small, two-bed dorm room. Marc could only stand back and watch as four nosy women each contributed their own special opinion as to what was necessary to set up the room according to what each of us felt was right for my son and his roommate.

"No, Mom, Aunt Faye is right to place my bookcase on the other wall."

"Jan, there isn't enough room to squeeze by the desk to get to the bathroom."

"Let's stop all the fuss and get to the 5 & 10 to pick up hangers."

By the time we were finished, Marc was thrilled to bid us farewell, even though we were reluctant to leave. Such is the pain of letting go for a parent, grandparent and great-aunt.

During the summer of 1984, each boy had a summer job at camp or was off visiting an exchange student somewhere abroad. Mom filled in while I vacationed for a couple of weeks in Finland, to meet Marc's second exchange student's family. Kalle's mother, Irya and I became instant soul-sisters. Life in Helsinki was in sharp contrast to Japan, as everyone in Kalle's family spoke English.

One of the highlights of this trip was travelling to Leningrad for a week with Irya. We marveled at the deprivations the Russians faced in this desolate capital city. As we investigated food markets and residential complexes, both of us were appalled at the lack of modern conveniences so readily found in our respective countries but we marveled at the Hermitage and many other official buildings.

Irya was an excellent tour guide as we wandered along designated tourist paths. My biggest surprise came on the day I went flying out of the bathtub and landed on the floor of the bathroom, having slipped on a bar of soap. Fortunately, I escaped with a few scratches and all of my bones intact. All in all, we made the best of our surroundings and enjoyed our time there before heading back happily to Finland.

Before commencing my second year at school in the fall, Roy was transported to Hofstra University in Long Island by Aunt Fay and me. It was quite a comical scene as we literally dumped him off with his trunk at a dorm but dared not leave our car. Other football players from the team were lounging in front of the building and Roy flipped out of the back seat, grabbed his trunk, and barked out his orders before we could say a word.

"Don't get out of the car, Mom," he hissed. "Just drive quietly away. I'll handle this."

I saluted and sped off while the tears came tumbling down and Aunt Fay tried to comfort me. Letting go and moving on is not as easy as it sounds.

Ding-a-Ling!

IN 1985, WITH MY TWO OLDEST SONS living away from home in college, our Friday night after-dinner scene was played out by my remaining three sons. As soon as we got up to begin our clean-up chores, Rex took this as his signal to dive under the table to slurp up any scraps of food that might have fallen from lips or napkins. The job chart dictated that Brian and Glenn would either stack dishes in the dishwasher, wash down the kitchen table or take out the trash. Although they alternated these tasks, Glenn's moaning never wavered.

"Mom, can't I please come home tonight from our gang meeting at eleven instead of ten-thirty? I'm the only one who has to leave early to walk home to make your deadline and it breaks up our meeting every time!"

"When you're 16, we'll revisit that request," I said, rather perfunctorily, as usual.

"Oh, Mom, that's so unfair!"

He growled the same way each time, as he left the kitchen in a huff. Once both boys had departed for their Friday night ritual gatherings with friends, that left Rex and me to enjoy a peaceful, quiet evening of relaxing, especially for me after a busy week of law school.

One particular Friday night, a shocking telephone call interrupted my favorite TV show.

"I'd like to speak to Janet Felgoise," the caller said.

"This is she," I said. "Who's calling?"

"Miss, this is Sergeant Stevens from Lower Moreland Township Police Department and I'm requesting that you come down to the station, immediately to pick up your son, Glenn."

"What? What happened to him? Is he okay? Can I speak to him now?"

The questions kept pouring out of me.

"He's safe, Mrs. Flegoise, and we'll explain it all when you come down."

"I'll be right there!"

I was shaking with disbelief and immediately called my neighbor.

"Maureen, I know it's after ten, but please, you must drive me to the police station, as they are holding Glenn there. I don't know why, not yet."

We arrived in a few minutes and were escorted into a small reception room by Sergeant Stevens.

"Please relax," he said, "I know this is an upsetting time, but I want to assure you that everyone is safe and there were no injuries. Our squad car apprehended a vehicle containing five teenagers, and your son, Glenn, was among the passengers. We received numerous complaints from the neighbors in your development that their doorbells were being rung. When they went to open their front doors, they saw a white car speeding off. It was rather easy for the patrol car on duty to locate the white car, driving along the streets in the Albildale development. The Captain is waiting for the other parents to arrive to issue disorderly disturbance citations to them, too. By the way, the driver of the run-away vehicle was licensed to drive!"

Glenn's wailing cries during our return trip home in Maureen's car could be heard throughout every street we passed as he sobbed, non-stop!

"I'm so sorry, Mom, we never expected anyone would call the police. It was such a bad, stupid idea, I'll never do it again, I promise!"

"You bet you'll never have a chance to do it again."

I put on my best stony face, while I saw Maureen sporting a motherly smirk.

Glenn never realized my great relief that the "Doorbell Ringing Incident" resulted in no serious injury, car accident or damage to property. However, there were three positive results from this potentially scary incident.

First, his participation in the episodic retelling turned out to be a hilarious scene we recalled for many years. It also established my role as his savior, whose legal acumen prevented a jail term.

(The crime: ringing doorbells?)

Lastly, it created a much calmer end to Friday night dinners for the four of us, because Glenn's dramatic scenes were eliminated.

You see, he patiently waited until his sixteenth birthday until he dared bring up a single request for a new Friday night curfew.

*Jan's Brushes
with History*

Part 2

The Assassination
November 22, 1963

I WAS SITTING IN THE TEACHERS' LOUNGE at Elkins Park Jr. High where I has been teaching history for four years. No one was paying any attention to the TV, which was playing someone's favorite soap opera. I casually perused *The Philadelphia Inquirer* for a few minutes until the next period bell rang.

Suddenly, all four teachers froze.

"We interrupt this program to announce that President John F. Kennedy has been shot during his motorcade drive through the city of Dallas, Texas. He has been rushed to the nearest hospital for treatment."

We crowded around the TV, breathlessly tuned to every word spoken by the announcer. Just then, our principal entered the lounge.

"Listen up folks, I just learned that the President just died in the emergency room of the hospital. I need some help making a decision."

"He's dead? Are you sure? We just heard he had been shot."

"Yes, I heard the latest, right before I entered," he said. "Listen, I need your input. It's now after two p.m. and school will be dismissed at three. Should I make this announcement over the PA system to tell the kids or let them go home without knowing about this tragedy? At home, their parents will tell them."

We all started talking at once, incredulous, shocked, and trying to come to terms with it.

"Wait a minute," he said, "I can't hear you all at once. One at a time, please."

"If we're too upset to handle this and the news is too devastating for the kids to handle, let's not make any revelations. Let their parents comfort them more easily, at home."

"I agree," I said, trying to regain my composure. "If we're this upset, can you imagine how the kids are going to react and we won't have time to comfort them before dismissal."

A consensus was quickly reached, and the Principal thanked us for helping him make the right decision. As the bell rang to announce the last class of the day, I gathered my books, wiped my tears and exited for my room, concealing my heartache and shock. I felt heroic being able to conceal my grief until dismissal without giving away the tragedy that befell America that day.

The Assassin Is Murdered
November 23, 1963

ON THAT SATURDAY AFTERNOON, Bert and I were still glued to the TV set in our new apartment, watching the news of how the police captured the alleged assassin, Lee Harvey Oswald. We witnessed the procession as he was being transferred from one section of the Dallas City Hall jail to another.

To say that we were overwhelmed by the constant barrage of television watching since the horrific events of Thursday would be an understatement. Yet, we just couldn't seem to get enough of the current events, which had been taking place in real time right before our eyes.

We witnessed the swearing in of Lyndon Johnson as the new President of the United States aboard Airforce I, as he stood next to Jackie Kennedy in her blood-stained pink suit and then the arrest of Oswald.

Now, we were glued to the latest blow-by-blow coverage as the camera panned right along with the police moving Oswald through the jailhouse. The corridor they walked him through was surrounded by news reporters, police and officials.

Then, shots rang out!

We were first-hand witnesses to his demise by an apparent observer in the crowd, a man named Jack Ruby. This was no episodic TV series. We were shocked, minute by minute, by what we were watching as live witnesses to the death of JFK's assassin.

We kept screaming in disbelief at the chaos and apprehension of Jack Ruby. Who was he? Was it even possible to digest any more shocking footage after all we'd been exposed to in the past 48 hours?

After observing Ruby's apprehension and Oswald's body being whisked away to a nearby hospital, we turned off the TV. We desperately needed relief from the non-stop visual nightmares we had been subjected to—real history, not your typical TV fiction—right there in our living room!

Why I Ignored the Civil Rights Movement August 1963

BETWEEN THE EARLY AND LATE SIXTIES, I was pre-occupied with raising babies (one miscarriage and four deliveries within five years). I had no spare time to pay much attention to events going on outside of my own domestic orbit. The first time I even took stock of national movements or politics was when my sixty-something-year-old in-laws (who I considered old timers back then) announced they were participating in the Civil Rights March on Washington in August of 1963.

Our synagogue, Temple Judea, had ordered buses to transport congregants to join Rev. Martin Luther King, Jr.'s march for Civil Rights. Harris and Dottie Felgoise were the first to sign up to go. I was so impressed and a little envious, I must admit. Since I wasn't really involved in life outside my home. I lacked information and interest about the impetus for this movement, which had been sweeping the country.

Just getting through a typical day of nurturing, teaching and tending to three boys under the age of three was enough of a challenge. I was so absorbed in mothering that I had little time for anything else and didn't even realize I was missing anything, let alone something as monumental as the Civil Rights movement.

The evening of the August March, I watched the TV coverage and wondered what I might have done if I didn't have baby duty. Would I have become a part of that entourage? I couldn't have answered that question because political, social and national life was so far removed from my private life during those years.

The most I could do was applaud all the participants of every religion and race who spoke out by being present to support the momentum that was beginning to change life in America.

An Astronaut Lands on the Moon
July 21, 1969

BERT AND I WERE RECLINING IN BED around two in the morning after being glued to the TV screen all night. We both felt like we were on the team of Mission Control, absorbed by the minutia of reporting the final minutes of the moon landing by Apollo II, the first spaceship to ever reach that goal.

"I think we should wait until the landing is eminent before we wake the boys," Bert said.

"Okay, let's roll," I ordered, "it'll take some time to get them wide awake to know what's going on."

We made a bee line into the boys' rooms. I gathered up Roy, almost three years old and Bert retrieved Marc, who was four. We carried our sleepy bundles back into our bedroom and huddled together in our king-sized bed. I was correct about the boys' lack of cognitive skills since being taken to a dark room where the only light was shining brightly from the TV screen. They were still out of it and barely awake.

"This is it, guys, one of the most exciting adventures of your lifetimes," Bert said. "We're watching our spacecraft land on the moon!"

"Where's the moon, Daddy?" Roy said.

"Why, way up in the sky," Bert said. "Look, the hatch is opening, and an astronaut is getting ready to climb down the ladder of the Shuttle to walk on the moon."

"This is amazing, isn't it?" I said. "We wanted you both to see it happen!"

"Uh huh," Marc mumbled, rubbing his eyes.

After being mesmerized for hours watching this unfold, we were ecstatic with energy and wonder at the sight of the surface of the moon and the first steps Neil Armstrong slowly took.

Then Bert and I roared out loud as we caught sight of two sleeping bundles cuddled in our bed.

"Well, we didn't want them to miss this 'historic' moment, even though we interrupted their sleep!"

The joke was on us as naive parents as "historical" quickly became "hysterical" when we realized our expectations were overblown!

Nixon Resigns
August 8, 1974

BERT'S OFFICE WAS LOCATED behind our children's playroom and the laundry room of our home in Huntington Valley. On this particular summer day, it was over-crowded with family members, occupying the sofa and the additional chairs we had brought in to watch television as President Richard Nixon delivered his resignation speech.

Harris and Dottie Felgoise, my in-laws, along with my brother Joel and his wife, had joined Bert and I to take in the spectacle. Our attention was captured by my father-in-law's reactions. We tried to stifle our laughter, watching in disbelief as he sat there crying, watching Nixon speak! Harris was aware of our giggling and ignored our comments, as he kept his attention on the TV. He had purposefully moved his chair right in front of the TV, as if to ignore our snickering and completely tune us all out. We knew he was an ardent Nixon fan, but this show of support was too much to bear.

Marc, our nine-year-old, was the only child in the room, sitting on the floor, munching on a carrot. Suddenly, he started coughing and then the sounds grew louder in intensity. He was choking! Joel was the first to recognize his distress and jumped up to hold Marc upside down by his feet to try to dislodge the obstruction.

We all stood up to help, except Harris, who was intently focused on the screen and purposely ignored the excitement. He must have thought we were joking again about him. Although Joel's efforts relieved Marc's distress, Bert want to have him checked out at Holy Redeemer Hospital and they soon departed for the short drive down Huntingdon Pike.

Harris, still glued to the TV with his back to us, remained so focused on Nixon's farewell that he was completely oblivious to the drama which had just unfolded. If we thought his actions were humorous *before* our little drama, we started to roar with laughter, this time with a big load of relief mixed in.

He purposely had no clue about what we had just gone through and couldn't believe it when we told him what he had missed!

Three Mile Island Blows Up
March 28, 1979

OUR FAMILY'S FIRST SKI ADVENTURE in Park City, Utah, was induced by the airlines' price war featuring the "Kids Fly Free" campaign. As the parents of four children, that was an offer we couldn't afford to pass up, so off we flew. We felt fortunate that we also had cousins to visit during our off hours from the slopes, so all systems were set to go.

We enjoyed our ski lessons, which we all desperately needed, especially me! Although we had experimented with skiing excursions in the Poconos, the height of the mountain regions in the West were beyond our expectations and abilities. Glenn at age nine, continuously slid backward because the angles of the slopes were so dramatic.

By the time we came close to the end of our vacation, we all recognized significant strides as skiers, and we kept congratulating ourselves with our accomplishments. Of course, the teenagers made the most advances as they slushed their way down the beginner's slopes.

The day before we were ready to depart for home, we learned of a catastrophic event in our home state of Pennsylvania. There had been a partial "meltdown" in the nuclear power plant located near Harrisburg. This resulted in the emission of radioactive gases into the atmosphere, so that over one hundred and forty thousand people had to be evacuated from the area. We were soon notified that planes weren't flying into this east coast region.

"Jan, don't even think about flying home until it is cleared for approval," my mother said.

"Come on, gang," Bert said, "we're going to fly west to California and visit cousin Evelyn for a few days until final approval about safety is announced."

Off we flew to Los Angeles and extended our Easter vacation from school. We also blew through our vacation budget, as there were no money promotions for flights to LA! At this time, no one understood just what a nuclear meltdown signified or the phenomenal cost of one billion dollars for the clean-up, which was finally completed in 1993.

Our vacation savings plan was certainly challenged by events beyond our control. What was so coincidental was the release of the movie, *China Syndrome* that same month, featuring Jane Fonda and Michael Douglas, about an accident in a power plant. Had we seen that film, we might have treated the situation more seriously than we did, as we lacked the informational perspective at the time to really understand the dangerous potential of the accident.

LAW SCHOOL?
ARE YOU KIDDING?

How, When and Why
I Decided to Become a Lawyer

MY DECISION TO BECOME A LAWYER was the direct result of witnessing my husband's heart attack in the middle of the night, which left me a single mom of four boys, alone to face the repercussions of an unimaginably horrible trauma. What some people called a "preposterous" decision began a challenging sags that would change the course of my life. After all, who would hire a rookie lawyer who started law school at age 45?

Surviving the pain and anxiety of making the funeral arrangements turned out to be mere grist for the mill of events which followed. During the many months of wrangling in law offices to conclude negotiating with banks and mortgage representatives, I became more and more intrigued by the process of law and the people who practiced it. My grief eventually became secondary to the peripheral immersion I was forced to experience as I navigated my way through a barrage of legal issues pertaining to Bert's law practice.

"Elaine, you can't leave in the middle of closing Bert's law practice to work for his friend Samuel. As his legal secretary, you're the only one who knows all the cases and the clients. Please stay aboard."

"Rick, if the law firm's client files aren't returned from your new employer by tomorrow afternoon, I'm filing an ethics action with the Bar Association."

Yes, that was me talking to my husband's secretary, a suburban housewife suddenly thrown into an unexpected legal mess. I had barely finished sitting shiva when I was bombarded with legal maneuvering to extricate our home from the financial collateral entanglement of the housing construction loan. To my surprise, my interest in how my legal team kept one step ahead of the bank posse became intriguing. Finally, after months of numerous financial meetings, all the legal challenges were concluded, and our family home was safely secured.

Amidst this drama and chaos, another scene played out, which stimulated my future career path. The elderly and dignified attorney representing me jolted my sensibilities with his response to my new idea of possibly entering the legal profession.

"Jan, you'll do just fine as a paralegal," he said.

"John, I don't think you got my message. I'm thinking about entering law school."

That was it. I had thrown down the gauntlet and become "Jan of Arc," a woman on a mission, determined to attend law school!

I enlisted two women lawyers I was close to test my sanity about my new resolution. Judy Novins Brown was my brother Joel's first girlfriend in college. Twenty years later, she was right there next to me, offering her supportive rationale for how I could fulfill my plans, which meant so much to me. Naomi Gerber Eichen, my high school and college best friend, was a New Jersey attorney.

"Don't worry, Jan, you have my time and support, and if things get shaky, you'll have my kick in the pants to propel you forward."

With these two endorsements from women who had made it into the legal profession in the '60s and '70s, I felt firm in my resolve to get started.

"Easier said than done," goes that famous expression.

First, I had to catch up with reality and discover just what was involved in the whole process of going to law school. I set up appointments with a friend and an acquaintance, both vice deans at their respective law schools, Villanova and Temple. Arnie, with whom I had a closer connection, took me on a tour of Villanova's Law School facilities.

"Let's sit in on a few classes together, Jan, so you can get a sense of the student body composition and how things feel."

I was grateful for that research.

Marjorie Lawrence, the wife of the former Lt. Governor of Pennsylvania, with whom Bert had a nice connection, offered me a warm and gracious welcome to Temple Law School. As soon as I surveyed the students passing me in the new facility housing the law school, I was ready.

"Dean Lawrence," I said, "this is the place for me. The mix of ages, shapes, colors and sexes is resonating with me right away. When I compare it to the other facility I visited, I'm convinced that Temple is where I want to be."

Marjorie was delighted while Arnie was in total disbelief when I informed him.

"You're choosing Temple over us?"

"Yep, the diversity there impressed me and won my vote. Besides, I noted that there are quite a few older students in Temple's classes, which makes all the difference to me."

Arnie shook his head incredulously, but I was still grateful for his support.

Although I might have been secure in my decision about which school to attend, I was still a long way from getting accepted. I had a great challenge ahead of me just to get into gear and engage in the application process. That meant orienting my brain, which hadn't been used for studying since I earned a master's degree in education 17 years earlier.

I slaved away at it, studying as much as I could to prepare for the LSAT exams. For me, it was matter of sheer determination and guts, which led to my eventual achievement.

When my acceptance letter to Temple University Law School arrived in the spring of 1983, I was deliriously happy for the first time in a year. I was on my way to disproving all the nay-sayers, and even better, earning a law degree at the age of 48.

Surfing the Shocks

WITH ONE SON SAFELY ENSCONCED at college for his freshman year, and *only* three at home to contend with, all my attention shifted to prepare for my inaugural steps as a law student. A few weeks before classes began, I coincidentally met a neighbor, Marilyn Walder, who was also matriculating as a first-year law student. As "mature" students, we both felt more powerful having an ally to face such unforeseen challenges.

My first few days as a law student saw my over-confident attitude about handling everything I encountered, melt away very quickly. When the time came to develop a study schedule, I felt totally incompetent, which shocked me. It had been more than 17 years since I'd completed my master's degree course work and I was positively out of practice.

I now had to share my nighttime study obligations with Roy, Brian and Glenn—at prescribed times—as I met each of each privately to review their work. They didn't quite know how to react to a mother who was as busy as they were with homework. Although we stationed ourselves in different spots we carved out throughout the house, we had no problem yelling out to each other when we needed consulting or connecting.

"Mom, you were supposed to be revising my French outline fifteen minutes ago."

"Okay, I'll be right down."

"Hey, Mom, then you'll be late to help me at 9:30."

"What about me?"

The voices seemed to be coming from everywhere. Somehow, all the test preparations were reviewed, and the homework schedule shifted, rebalanced and accommodated all four Felgoise students in the house.

Roy glided through his senior year. On Sundays, he toured the colleges that had committed to offering him a football scholarship after scouting his high school games. The coach from Hofstra University charmed us the most before Roy confirmed his decision to play for him.

Brian buckled down each night to meet the demands of his tenth-grade teachers after spending each afternoon in football practice with Roy.

Glenn also practiced each day with his middle school sports teams and busied himself after dinner keeping up with his homework.

We were a busy (and hungry) household.

My most uninterrupted study time was in the afternoons. Whenever I could, I nestled on the couch with my fifth boy, Rex, our four-legged Springer Spaniel.

"Rex, I'm so happy to be spending this quiet study time alone with you this afternoon," I'd tell him, "before the gang arrives."

Our most joyous and literally delicious time began a few weeks later, after we began our wild adjustment to all the new classes and schedules, when I hired a chef. The young man arrived at our home to prepare dinner after completing his full-time job. We went wild with excitement and devoured all the unique recipes he conjured up for us. My sons had never before experienced such meals other than at restaurants, as I had inherited a limited menu repertoire from my mother, who always had a cook in the house.

Ecstatic with our new luck, we must have frightened him with our accolades and modest renumeration, because he departed after a couple of weeks. Alas, we sadly gulped down our disappointment as well as the humdrum TV dinners I resorted to serving. I marvel now, how my four six-footers maintained their growth spurts on such meager nutritional fare. This is my proof that genetics rule the roost.

Meanwhile, I was making good connections at school, where they boasted a relatively large number of "returning students" as we older "objects of suspicion" were referred to. That made it easy to make friends among our unique group amidst the larger selection of future lawyers. After sizing up the individual students, we and the other old-timers seemed to naturally cluster together according to maturity and wrinkles.

Although many first-year classes were conducted in lecture halls, we were also fortunately exposed to smaller classes taught by full professors. Our favorite, Professor Sonenshein always nattily groomed, formed a special bond with the older members of his class. When Brian became a law student at Temple Law eight years later, he was forced to correct an erroneous statement made by my favorite teacher.

"It's interesting to note a familiar name among this class roster," the professor said. "Mr. Felgoise, I believe that I taught your sister, a few years ago."

"Pardon me, sir, but that wasn't my sister; that was my mother!"

Brian's response lit up the classroom in peals of laughter.

The first shock I received about law school related to the large number of circular-shaped marks I collected during my initial set of mid-year final exams. I always prided myself on collecting triangular-shaped marks in both undergraduate and graduate school courses.

Although delighted to pass the stringent testing cycle of my first semester, I found a more challenging shock to contend with when the Women's Movement descended upon campuses in the 1980s. I had no experience with the vibrant anger, resentment and turbulence expressed by my younger female classmates.

"Did you hear what that bastard professor intimated?"

"No," I'd say, quite unsure what was being asked. "What are you talking about?"

I was a square from the 1950s, delighted to be surviving, comprehending and participating. I was completely oblivious to the female students' perceived slights, negative innuendos and sarcasm, which they believed emanated from male professors.

"Huh?" was all I could manage to mumble. I couldn't relate to their frustration and anger, which gushed forth in torrents of cursing at their lot as females in the class.

One day, I was paraded in front of the ladies' room mirror, where I was bullied into pretending to join the movement by learning how to put the four letters together in order to pronounce the "F" word. This was a milestone of the feminine mystique pervading law school.

My bigger achievement was in the classroom, where for the first time in my academic career, I wasn't even close to reaching the top of the class ranking. Thrilled to be just average, I carried on enough to survive my overwhelmingly challenging course work.

Much to my surprise, my first-year final exam scores didn't devastate me. The pride I felt in my accomplishment of remaining a viable student sustained me. Although the graduation date they cited sounded so far away from the end of my first year, I reached my first goal and continued onward as a student in good standing of The Class of 1986.

Spring Break in 1984 did not come soon enough, however, as all of us needed a vacation. We stuffed our station wagon and set out on a 1,200-mile trip down Route 95 to Orlando, Florida. Marc, Roy and I took turns driving the, careful to escape the scrutiny of each state's police force and arrived at Aunt Elaine and Uncle Lou's home near Disney.

At their restaurant, The Rusty Fox, we enjoyed the best food we'd had since our chef vanished. We were all happy to be vacationing together again and celebrating positive times.

Year Two: Even Better than the First

THE BEST PART OF STARTING my second year of law school was the confidence I felt marching back into those sacred halls. I exuded happiness and security with my many friendly classmates and even chose to enter the Moot Court competition.

Although I was not selected for such esteemed oral argument recognition, friends congratulated me for even entering the contest. I was developing a gutsy streak, aided by huge doses of tutorials, although I could never attain the levels exhibited by the younger female members of the student body.

On a few occasions, when the boys were home from school, I brought the two older ones with me so they could play hoops at lunch time with some of my male classmates, who were only five years older than my guys. I glided easily between the age groups and enjoyed a different connection with my professors than the typical student. As I felt more and more accepted and kept up my solid grades, a growing confidence led to my nascent participation in class recitations and reviews of material.

My excitement level soared when I obtained a seasonal job at the end of the school year for the summer of '85. I became a law clerk at a Bucks County firm, located about ten minutes from our house, run by a former state senator who had spent 20 years developing a large, multi-faceted practice with ten lawyers practicing personal injury, family law and trusts and estates. The office was housed in a large, one-story building with ample parking for attorneys and clients. I figured that I provided value to my employer because of my age and varied experience in leadership positions in the many organizations I had formerly participated in. Age and maturity gave me an advantage over most twenty-four-year-old second year law students and this firm recognized that immediately.

How short-sighted were the naysayers in their view of my future employment?

I won many law firm accolades for dealing with clients who confided in me and unloaded their stories. By the time I was ready to return to law school, I was offered a position at the firm upon graduation. I was exuberant, one of very few students who had a job offer before the last year of school even started. That distinction earned me some welcome bragging rights!

My boundless happiness was short-lived, however, when tragedy struck our family again. All five of us were settled back in school when Rex, our 15-year-old Springer Spaniel, suffered a stroke. Following Cookie, my first dog, Rex was the second I ever fell in love with and it was a long-term affair.

Just when our youngest son graduated into big boy pants and I put away the diapers and poopy messes forever, we found Rex. All six of us travelled to a small house in Philadelphia to check out this spirited, adult dog that my Aunt Rose and I had investigated earlier that day. All of us were smitten by this enthusiastically affectionate dog, who would not be contained.

I figured if I had four boys, ages four to almost nine, under reasonable control, then a dog should be no problem. But I had never met the likes of rambunctious, rollicking Rex of Kensington, his designated name on the pedigree papers.

Training him was an adventure.

After many years of "never say die" persistence, Rex finally stopped trying to jump up to kiss everyone's cheek. However, we were never able to diminish his penchant for slipping out of our home, whenever he sensed the slightest opening of any available door.

The moment his escape was noted, someone rang the cow bell at the garage door, announcing a Rex alarm! In our neighborhood, this became as significant as a fire drill. No matter what time of day, kids would pour out of their homes to assist the frantic Felgoise boys in rounding up Rex.

Invariably, he was lassoed and bag-tied and led home en masse by the posse. Head down, tail stub even lower, he would slink into the house and immediate banishment to the isolation chamber of the laundry room. In those days, there were no "time out chairs."

Rex contributed a great deal to further a sense of community within our block in Albidale, Huntingdon Valley. When the Rex Alarm bell clanged, he became everyone's dog!

Rex died in October at the vet's office and we brought his body home to a sacred burial ground. The two younger boys, now in high school, helped me bury Rex in our backyard, clandestinely, as it was surely contrary to township rules.

The boy's late note to school read, "Please excuse the lateness, as Brian and Glenn attended the funeral service for a friend."

For the rest of the year, Glenn and I scoured many SPCA's in our quest to save a life and adopt a Rex replacement.

Finally, in February of 1986, during my last semester in law school, we found "the one."

We dubbed her Jewel from the recent movie, *Jewel of the Nile*, a swashbuckling adventure flick. We brought this "Heinz 57" mongrel home to face an astonishingly negative, enraged onslaught from Brian.

"How could you have picked such a scruffy, dirtball, wirehaired excuse for a dog to bring home to this house?"

Of course, it didn't take long for her to work her way into his heart, although not to the same degree as ours.

Jewel faced many challenges at home, accommodating two new alpha leaders of her clan, when they returned from college during spring break.

"Just who are these two bozos trying to tell me what U can and cannot do?"

While she never said those exact words, she did soon learn to accommodate the steady stream of orders from her five human "friends," as we continued to train her during that summer vacation. However, these abrupt changes in her life didn't remotely prepare her for the shocking events she would ultimately experience four years later.

A Hero Returns

THE GREATEST CHALLENGE during my last two years of law school wasn't academic. It was gastronomic! Time for food prep was at a minimum so good old-fashioned TV dinners became my default menu of choice, much to the consternation of my two remaining boys at home.

After returning Marc and Roy to their respective colleges, I entered my last year at law school feeling like a triumphant Julius Caesar after conquering Egypt. I was a heroine returning with a job offer in hand for after graduation. I had been tested in the ultimate arena, not with academic studies but in the marketplace. The law firm had tested my mettle, determined my value to their organization and offered me a job with a respectable starting salary of $42,000. That propelled me to celebrity status, along with the handful of others who also returned after the summer as conquering heroes with job offers for the following year.

The irony was, I wasn't among the scholarly leaders of our class who were expected to land such a prize. Instead of pure brain power, it was my life experiences, maturity and a joie doe vivre personality, which had convinced my future employer to hire me.

My newly won fame made getting into my typical study mode a bit easier, that is until I was sidetracked by the appearance of Arthur. Although I had made a few male connections in the past year, I was too busy with family and school to get too interested.

Arthur was different. He wasn't a new person in my life. We had long history, beginning from the time we were third grade lovers. We were connected from the start, alphabetically, because of our last names, Goleman and Havsy, and became constant homeroom classmates all through junior and senior high school, even though we never really connected socially after the initial dazzle we enjoyed as little kids.

We met infrequently through the years after attending college and marrying our respective partners, mostly at planning meetings for our West Philly High School reunions.

Arthur and I were both widowed with children at the same stage in life. It was the bright idea of a mutual high school buddy to play Cupid and plot a reunion committee meeting to match us up. After a comfortable meeting of the minds, we developed a newfound friendship on a level we had never experienced. We commiserated over our similar feelings about our loss and problems with our children, my four and his two.

We met for fun excursions. As our friendship became more and more comfortable, we reassured each other through our respective crisis. I also benefited from

Arthur's accounting suggestions for my financial quandaries. Our relationship added another dimension of stability to my life because of his trusted, well-reasoned suggestion whenever I sought them. Everything was progressing smoothly until he suggested a change.

"Jan, I'm really enjoying our relationship and the connection I feel at this point, so I want to make a change."

"What do you mean?" I said. "We have so much fun together."

"I mean I want to develop a different level to our relationship because I've fallen in love with you."

I was overwhelmed, flattered and confused. Over the few months we had developed such a comfortable friendship, my nagging fear was the possibility of losing such a valued friend if our romance ever faltered. For days after Arthur's confession, I walked around like a drama queen, losing sleep and floundering in my studies. In great need of a practical opinion, I sought advice from a dear friend, Elaine.

"Are you crazy?" she said. "You already have the best friend part nailed down; the rest is topping on the cake. Don't be such an idiot, Jan; grab him!"

Fortified by her advice, Arthur and I worked out a slow-paced deal to see if our romantic inclinations were on the same level as our intellectual connection. All of the attributes so important to me in selecting a beau in my teens (I was married at 20) had become superficially inconsequential at my current stage of life.

Arthur's attributes—integrity, stability and cultural interests—were so compatible to my needs and desires that they overwhelmed my immature ideals of a "hunk." Elaine's kick in the pants did the trick and sent me over the goal line to solidify our deal. Instead of worrying about losing an important friend if our relationship didn't bloom the way we anticipated, I worked on the romantic factor and enabled it to easily blossom.

My last year of law school became a flurry of frantic, non-stop action. Between new activities in Brian's football arena, developing a special relationship and entering the work force before graduation, I was operating at a whole new level.

My future employer, Neil Hurowitz, at Astor Weiss, Kaplan & Mandel, asked me to accept a part-time job of 15 hours a week and I felt I could not refuse their request to continue my law-clerking. I joined the ranks of fellow students who proudly carried this banner of employment. It merely meant crunching my already jam-packed schedule as a parent and full-time student with a new love life.

Because of Brian's acclaimed athletic talents as the left- handed quarterback of the LM High football team, I also evolved into a cheerleader at every Saturday football game, home and away. Because our team wasn't exactly fulfilling its promise, I spent too many game with my eyes closed as the quarterback was continually tackled at the line of scrimmage. At this point in my life, catching my breath was sometimes literally a challenge all on its own.

Thank goodness the boys were as busy as I was and didn't notice—or at least pretended not to—how I barely kept the house together and kept them fed, at least well enough that they continued bulking up their bodies sufficiently to compete in their athletic endeavors.

What really bolstered their lives that year and helped me as a parent was the watchful eye of their amazing football coach, Mark Mason. It turned out that he was one of my students 20 years earlier at Elkins Park Junior High. He took a personal interest in the Felgoise boys and always reminded them of his connection and appreciation of their mom.

His leadership qualities instilled the value of good grades, hard work and dedication. I was so grateful for the extra effort he took to look out for Brian and Glenn during my last year of law school.

I'm still amazed we survived that crazy year and I'm sure it was made a lot easier because of the support I received from my proud fiancée, who never failed to encourage me.

Measuring Friends

There's an easy way to measure true friends.
Just add up the constant times they attend
To your problems and bolster your spirit,
And make sure that you'll have all the wit
For clearing up options clouding your mind
So you can follow your right path and find
The answers you seek to provide your peace
As that decision provides a new lease
On your life.

Expressions of true feelings for you
Are the easiest way to provide clues
About friends' loyalty and great concern,
Making it very easy to discern
Just how much you can trust and rely
On steadfast love, which they rarely deny,
While offering their unwavering belief
That you can provide your own relief
In your life.

So just wrap it up and call it a day.
You've found the formula and a sure way
To count your blessings; add up all your friends
Whose true relationships you'd never lend
Or carelessly toss away to the wind
By unkind words or those you'd rescind.
Enjoy their compassion and honesty
For friendships comprise all the poetry
Of your life.

From Tragedy to Triumph

JANUARY 28, 1986 was a catastrophic day for America. We had returned a few days earlier for our last semester as the Class of '86, and I must admit, many of us had a slightly blasé attitude by then after having met the challenge law school presented. The race for the best and finest had worn off and the emphasis for many of us was in securing a job for entry into the real world upon graduation. Professor Sonnenshine's large lecture hall was crammed with early morning sleepy students who were not terribly involved in his lecture.

Halfway through, I slipped out of my seat near the back of the amphitheater to use the ladies' room. On the way back to class, I saw large crowds gathered around a TV in the lobby, watching in horror as the tragic news about the spaceship Challenger flashed across the screen. Just 73 seconds after launching from Cape Canaveral in Florida the whole thing had exploded. The launch had gained special attention for weeks before because of Christa McAuliffe, a schoolteacher who had been selected to join the six astronauts.

I stood there spellbound, watching the continuously repeated pictures of the ghastly explosion. Shouts of anguished dismay were heard all around by mesmerized law students, frozen by the eerie details and images of such shocking devastation.

After a few moments, I re-entered the lecture hall, not knowing what to do. I wondered if I should relay the information to the class or remain silent. I scribbled a terse note at my seat, got up and approached the rostrum to hand it to the professor. Despite his surprised look as he saw me approaching, he hastily interrupted his lecture to glance at my note. In a solemn tone, he announced that the Commander Spaceship had just exploded upon take off. Groans, cries of disbelief, and hasty explanations erupted from the formerly inert group of more than 100 students. Class was abruptly dismissed as everyone leapt from their seats to find out more information. That terrifying event placed an indelible mark upon our last semester at Temple University Law School, never to be forgotten by any of us.

Graduation exercises were held across the street from our building on the university's basketball court. I had to purchase a few extra tickets to accommodate my family members from New York, Florida, and Los Angeles, who joined our usual cheering squad.

My hunt for tickets reminded me about my West Philadelphia High graduation, when I had to travel by trolley car the night before to buy two tickets from a classmate, who was working at a restaurant.

We practiced marching down the aisles and mounting the stairs to the podium, when our names would be announced for the presentation of diplomas. Some male class members marched in the procession carrying their young babies and small children. I decided that my four big babies would remain in the stands. Even if given the opportunity, we all knew they would never, ever, join the graduating parents and their progeny in a march for all to see.

A loud chorus of cheers erupted when I received my degree from the Dean, but it barely rose about the noise in such a large facility. My family grouping sat in the balcony under an umbrella of bobbing balloons, planned so I could spot them from my seat on the floor of the Palestra. After the ceremony, we proceeded to a local restaurant, where we wasted no time becoming a wild and wooly crowd with much to celebrate.

Our greatest party took place at the home of our dear friends, the Lemoles, who hosted us all in a spectacular, tented affair, held on the spacious grounds of their farmhouse in Huntingdon Valley.

Invitations were designed as replica subpoenas, ordering party goers to appear at the designated time by Order of the Montgomery County Court. The blue backing paper surrounding the Court Order was the exact paper used on all court documents.

Imagine the invited guests' surprise upon receiving a "Summons to Appear" to my graduation party. More than 100 guests dined and danced at this extravaganza to celebrate my hard-earned fame.

I was so honored to have such extraordinary hosts to entertain my guests and family at such a happy, celebratory event.

My new employer provided an unexpected comic element as he circulated among many new contacts and connections. He used the opportunity to meet and greet potential supporters in his bid for the fall primary election in his campaign for Pennsylvania State Senator. He even handed out campaign literature, as I stood by speechless, without any recourse.

Many friends and family members were enraged that he would use my party as his campaign stomping ground. My sons were eager to pick him up and expel him but jokes about his activity just peppered the event with more fun and giggles.

He was rewarded for his "faux pas" by ultimately losing his bid for re-election. When my sons learned about the election results, they cheered. I demurred, using my best lawyerly techniques of discretion.

The "Family" Law Degree

Bill Cosby pointed my path to Temple
"I could have gone anywhere" for law.
As an older mom, I reversed gears
Re-learning study skills, seeking advice
From four full-timers, my teen aged sons.
All student by day, we met at dinner
To share our life's events, then hit the books.
Souls were nursed in between pages,
No time for stroking psyches before bed.

This nighttime frenzy was but a calm,
Compared to my trepidation
Of making the 80's law school scene.
Legal study caused chaos in my life.
Fear of failure created tension
About classroom recitation: our answers
To professors' Socratic questions,
Designed to create budding legal minds,
My response seemed to me, mere sputter.

The cross-generational spirit failed
Between kids and the golden oldies.

JANET GOLEMAN FELGOISE

The Women's caustic views scared us,
We just couldn't subscribe to their anger,
We arrived and became liberal,
They stayed to become conservative.
But we cried en masse when the Challenger fell.
Legal research, Moot Court, briefs and exams
Etched their toll, testing the balance
I straddled, juggling my two worlds,
Of law student and part-time mother.

The completed first year, shored my resolve
I would survive the rest, with guts to spare.
Until I smashed into a scary question
I hadn't even dreamed about before.
Who would hire me at my advanced age?
This new landmine exploded my reality.
More needless worry piled upon the mound,
Of past panicked punches I had endured.
Relief was disguised as a job offer
Validating the value of maturity.

Agony relents after the Bar Exam.
This rite of passage makes lawyers of students.
Without success scores, one is doomed to repeat
The painstaking months to prepare again.
Finally, vindication was at hand,
A new lawyer was minted and stamped-out.
My sons exhaled their collective held breaths,
Whisking me to the mountain peak of pride.

Jan's Brushes
with History

Part 3

Spaceship Columbia Explodes January 28, 1986

I CAREFULLY LEFT MY SEAT in the middle of the lecture hall during my ethics class. On my way back after using the ladies' room, I noticed a large crowd in the foyer, riveted to a TV mounted on the wall. There was much excitement, nervous utterances and more people gathered by the minute.

"What's up?" I said, as I moved closer to the ever-expanding crowd of students.

"The Space Shuttle Challenger VII just exploded on takeoff!"

"Oh, my God!"

I didn't wait around for more details as I didn't want to miss any more time from this important lecture of my last semester of law school, so I headed for the classroom door. I stopped for a moment to consider what I should do upon entering the hall.

Should I quietly take my place and resume notetaking where I left off, as if nothing had happened, or should I walk down to the professor's podium and inform him of this national calamity?

I made a split-second decision and descended the steps to the ground level of the room and approached the lectern. The professor looked up as I approached, stopped talking and stepped to the side to greet me.

"I'm sorry to interrupt, but on my way back to class, I saw a crowd gathering in front of the TV monitor just outside. The Challenger Space Shuttle has just exploded on takeoff from Canaveral!"

The shocked look on his face was immediately apparent to the class, who were waiting intently to know what was going on. They could feel that something serious had occurred.

"I don't know if you want to announce it right now to the class or not," I said, "but I wanted you to know immediately."

"Thanks for advising me. I will cancel the class right away and explain why."

Cries of alarm and anguish exploded throughout the room when Professor Eisner announced the tragedy. There had been such extensive news coverage of a schoolteacher joining the astronaut team for the first time on this mission, which only enhanced the excitement of this recent takeoff. It certainly added to my classmates' emotional reaction to this great loss.

Friends gathered around me as we departed together to find more information from the latest news reports in the hall adjoining the lecture hall.

My decision to report or not troubled me for days following the incident. I believed I had made the right choice to allow my class to share in the national tragedy as it was occurring. It was another monumental event that we would long remember and exactly where we were when we first learned the terrible news.

WHEN EVERYTHING OLD IS NEW AGAIN

True Love

MY FIRST ROMANTIC LOVE AFFAIR wasn't a classic "affair" because it occurred when I was in third grade. Sadly, I had to share my heart's desire with Ilene and Walda, my best friends. We plotted constantly, during morning and afternoon recess, which were just about the only chances we had to corral Arthur, the boy of our dreams, with his dark hair and bushy eyebrows. Since he could easily escape our kisses after school, that left us no other option to satisfy our innocent lust.

"Janet, you stay near the school yard door and start chasing him when he comes out." Walda said. "Ilene and I will wait in the school yard and he'll run into us."

"What happens if Arthur doesn't come out?" I said.

"Of course, he'll come out," Ilene said. "Stop being silly, Janet."

No matter how we planned, Arthur always escaped our clutches and our strategies to capture him never panned out. The three of us were only willing to share our prized target because we knew that none of us had the courage to chase him alone. But by sixth grade, I was busy on my own pursuing other lovers without having to run after anyone. We did all of our kissing without exhausting ourselves at spin-the-bottle parties.

By the time I graduated high school, Arthur was totally off my radar screen as we marched onward to colleges, careers and marriages. He and I kept in touch periodically as we both helped to organize class reunions.

Fast forward forty years, when I was widowed and received a telephone call one day from a mutual friend.

"Jan, we're planning our next reunion," Alan said, "so Arthur will pick you up and bring you to my house for a meeting."

"I thought it wasn't until next year."

"We're starting early. Remember our disaster at the last celebration because we didn't have enough planning time?"

I had no idea what Alan was up to, that he was acting as Cupid to make the connection for Arthur and me, two committee members, to get together under the pretext of a reunion meeting. Since we were old friends, it felt natural enough to spend the ensuing months catching up and sharing our respective widow/widower experiences and how we were handling our new roles in life. Our relationship was friendly and welcomed but it wasn't romantic. I was too busy raising four teen-age boys while attending my last year of Temple Law School.

That changed when Arthur told me he wanted something much more than a friendship. I didn't know what to do and felt almost as clueless as I was back in third grade. Thank God for faithful girlfriends.

"Elaine," I said, acknowledging my cluelessness, "I need some good advice."

"What's up, Jan?"

"Arthur wants to get serious and change our platonic relationship!"

"That's great! What kind of advice could you possibly need about that?"

"I don't know what to do."

"What do you mean? Are you crazy? Or just nuts? He's such a great guy!"

"Suppose the romance part doesn't work out. I'm afraid I'll lose such a good friend."

"Now I know you are crazy! Do you realize what a "find" you have? If you're starting out as good friends, it can only get better! Call him back right now!"

"Are you sure?"

"I'm really sure and so are you!"

She wasn't kidding. I made two telephone calls after I hung up with Elaine. The first one was to my mother.

"Hi Mom, could you do me a favor?

"Sure, dear, what do you need?"

"Well, it's almost spring break from law school and Arthur and I want to go away for that weekend. Could you come over and stay with the boys while I'm away?"

"Oh . . ."

"Mom?"

"How far away are you going?"

"Host Farm, right in Lancaster."

"Well, Jan, I'll come on one condition."

"Are you kidding? What, Mom?"

"I'll stay with the boys to make sure there are no parties and they don't wreck the house, if you promise me one thing."

"Sure."

"Promise me that if you see any one I know at the resort during that getaway weekend, you will not say hello to them!"

"Mom, what are you talking about? This is 1986, not 1936!"

I agreed to her terms and Arthur and I had a wonderful weekend.

After surviving our own personal tragedies, a pair of life-long good friends finally became lovers, got married and blended two families totaling six kids in a new home. Our dog and their cat just added to the hilarious times we shared.

Between Ilene and Walda and me, I was the one who had the last laugh. I was certainly the lucky one, who finally caught Arthur and nailed him with a kiss.

The Great Proposal of 1987

THE DINING ROOM TABLE for our 1987 Thanksgiving feast was extended to its limits to accommodate my beau, Arthur H. Havsy, and his two children, my four sons, my mother, mother-in-law, and Uncle Hank and Aunt Desna. Aunt Fay and Cousin Sandy arrived just in time for dessert.

"What took so long?" everyone said. "You missed the best turkey dinner."

"Don't worry," I said, "we saved the sweetest part for you, guys."

"Squeeze together everyone, so they fit in."

While all my dear family and friends were busy devouring a menu of fancy pies, cakes and delicacies contributed by our guests, I ran into the kitchen, grabbed my Thanksgiving surprise and re-entered the party carrying a very large sign.

ARTHUR, WILL YOU MARRY ME?

A hidden camera would have captured a table-full of slack jaws, wide eyes and spontaneous exclamations of surprise at this dramatic moment. Especially when Arthur uttered, his priceless response.

"No way, Jan, you missed your chance when you declined my earlier proposal!"

The room exploded in raucous laughter, accompanied by foot stomping. Then, with a wide grin, Arthur rose from his seat and caressed me.

"Only kidding, dear," he said, "I'd love to marry you."

Wild cheers came from all around the table.

"Ladies and gentlemen, sons and daughter, help me toast this special moment with a sip of Dom Perignon," I exclaimed with wild excitement.

I produced the prized bottle of champagne, which we savored to toast our joy. The excitement and rush of adrenalin lasted until the last person departed, who was of course, Arthur, my sweetheart, my one and only third-grade lover.

Felgoise-Havsy Fun and Games

THE COMEDIC SCENE AT THANKSGIVING was easily matched at our wedding the following June. We decided on a family-only affair with just close relatives and out of town guests for our ceremony, to be followed by a luncheon for friends at the Barclay Hotel on Rittenhouse Square. The night before our wedding, Arthur and I opted for the height of luxury in a three-bedroom honeymoon suite, as there were so many out of town relatives staying at our homes.

"Aren't we lucky to be chasing each other around this three-bedroom suite at the Barclay? We're the first couple to share our honeymoon suite the night before our wedding," I murmured.

"Jan, we had no choice, there were so many out of town guests staying at our homes, there was no room for us!" Arthur laughed.

With our families lining both sides of a small, flower-festooned room, I marched down the aisle on the arm of my brother, Joel, who proudly gave me away. Seated among the guests were my special relatives, the Suuitarinans, who traveled from Finland to attend their honorary sister's wedding. Joel guided me to the chuppah, the Jewish ceremonial canopy, with each one of my four sons holding a pole to support it. I joined Arthur under the tent with Jeff and Lynne Havsy as we all stood before the rabbi, thoroughly excited.

Joel whispered one of his typical cute remarks to Brian, who tried valiantly to stifle his giggling response.

"No way, Uncle Jose."

His attempts to subdue his laughter led to hiccups, which induced mimicking, convulsive motions among his three brothers, trying to diffuse their own laughter. One of the boys erupted in a giggle, which caused a ripple of laughter that spread quickly to the other three, who tried to suppress their reaction. The more they tried to restrain themselves, the more their bodies convulsed with laughter. This began to affect the poles they were holding, and they wobbled more and more with each spontaneous convulsion.

Arthur and I were mesmerized as we listened intently to the rabbi, so we weren't aware of the ruckus going on around us with the swaying chuppah, until we saw the rabbi's facial expression suddenly change. He looked flushed, like he'd never encountered such a thing!

We held our collective breath until the boys' heaving subsided and they regained control of the poles and the fabric hanging precariously over our heads. Then the rabbi continued the ceremony and managed to complete it without any more unexpected frivolity.

As we triumphantly marched back down the aisle as Mr. and Mrs., the guests released their pent-up laughter about this bouncing "topper" episode, which they repeated to others, many times, I am sure of that.

Arthur and I didn't move into our new home until after we returned from a fabulous honeymoon. When Arthur's daughter, Lynne, set off for summer camp, we boarded the Princess Line's *Love Boat* for a trip from California to Alaska, which was the first cruise for both of us. The combination of dining at the Captain's Table and the adventures we had touring Anchorage and made for a honeymoon that blew our fuses. The passengers were thrilled to meet and congratulate the first 50-year-old honeymooners they had ever known, as we were a rarity in those days. Alaska was unforgettable, including the thrill of watching a pod of whales swim by our 600-passenger ship in these early days of the cruise.

Move-in day to 130 Fisher Road, Jenkintown, PA, the new home of the eight-membered Felgoise-Havsy families was in September 1988.

The Felgoise boys occupied three bedrooms on the third floor. Roy and Glenn shared the largest room and Marc and Brian were assigned to their own bedrooms. Jeff and Lynne had the two bedrooms on the second floor, while Arthur and I floated around the master bedroom, connected to our den by a master bath.

Marc had graduated from college the year before and Roy graduated that summer. Jeff left for his second year at Lehigh University, Arthur's alma mater; Glenn departed for the University of South Florida, and Brian headed for the University of Pittsburgh after a year at the Naval Academy Prep School. Lynne luxuriated in her purple bedroom with an attached bath and attended Germantown Friends School as a sophomore.

Everyone fit into his or her preordained slots except our respective pets. Scratchy, the Havsy's cat, scared our dog, Jewel, with her menacing hisses whenever the two bumped into each other. Jewel ran in fear, desperate to save herself from the ferocious sounds of her feline nemesis. My go-to animal naturalist, Jane Lemole, assured us that the antagonism between our respective pets would evolve into a real companionship, in time.

Surely but slowly, the five human occupants and two animals who lived together acclimated to the rhythms, responsibilities and spaciousness of our three-story, seven-bedroom, Tudor home. Arthur and I were thrilled to be the proud owners of this beautiful, spacious 1920's show place and believed intuitively that everything had worked out, just as Jane had promised.

Animals teach us the most interesting lessons. In less than a month, Scratchy and Jewel bonded! They followed each other the two flights of steps up to the third-floor bachelor pad, while the two collegians were away. They supped from each other's dishes and even occasionally napped near each other.

For the first time, we realized how each of our family's pets demonstrated the typical characteristics associated with the other's nature. Scratchy was always sashaying up close and personal to investigate the humans' activities while Jewel exhibited her stand-offish, "I'll be around when I'm ready" attitude.

We Felgoises had not recognized her aloof, solitary nature when she was the only animal around our home. Scratchy, to the contrary, was the inquisitive, pesky feline, always moseying around, looking for action. At our new home, we always had to call Jewel to join a family activity, while Scratchy loved to adorn Arthur's lap to seek his petting strokes as she moved around to find a comfortable spot. Jewel would doze in another room, oblivious to this freely offered affection!

Seeing how our respective pets adjusted to each other's temperament, habits and personalities, without speaking a word to each other, gave us great inspiration.

We gathered our collective group of six children together during the fall college break for an important family conference. Using our pet's resolution of acceptance and new camaraderie as the example to be followed, we laid down the law of 130 Fisher Road. If our respective pets could achieve a new harmony without talking each other's language, so could our two diverse groups of children!

One caveat: be advised that we, their parents, were *never* going to get involved with their issues to settle arguments or straighten out any differences.

"Don't even contemplate approaching us to resolve your disagreements," we said. "It's not going to happen."

Henceforth, they were on their own to follow our "dog and cat game" and work-out their own problems. Our firm stance was tested on a few occasions, but our resolve to disengage from our children's entanglements never faltered.

The Scratchy/Jewel psychology won the day and the lovers' parental relationship wasn't held hostage by engaging in resolving any of their respective children's disagreements.

When two parents agree on a strategy, good things will happen.

How a Dog and a Cat Tamed a House of Strangers

ALTHOUGH ARTHUR AND I MARRIED in June, we didn't move into our new home in Jenkintown until September, once we'd gotten the kids off to their respective colleges.

"I'm exhausted," I said to Arthur, after shipping out Glenn and Brian.

"I know, Hon, I only had Jeff to send back to school and it was hard work. Now we have to adjust to having Marc and Roy, our two college graduates, settle into their rooms on the third floor, while Lynne lives on the second floor next to us."

"We were so lucky to find a seven-bedroom palace to combine our families," I said.

Indeed, we were, but it wasn't only humans we needed to settle in our new home. Our family were moving into what would become their new home, too.

In an effort to do it as smoothly as possible, we decided to "house break" them one at a time and Jewel won the lottery. Although she was comfortable in my two-story home, it took her time to get used to climbing an additional flight of steps to join the boys on the third floor. This extra level, however, provided her a much-needed sanctuary in the days to come.

"Well, here she goes," I murmured as I opened the door to our new home. Jewel, our wheat colored, scruffy coated canine, pranced inside and eagerly sniffed around. There was a lot of ground for her to cover as she tiptoed around the first floor, eyeing her favorite, familiar furniture and inspecting some new replacements.

"What's going on here?"

We speculated on what she must be thinking.

"There are new chairs around the dining room table and the den sofas are arranged differently in a larger room. What happened to the drapes that matched the living room chairs?"

These questions turned out to be easy enough for Jewel, but it was a different story when Scratchy, the Havsy feline, came to reside with us in the following days. When the two animals met for the first time it was quite a drama. Jewel's reaction to Scratchy's menacing hisses sent her yelping in a panic to find safety upstairs.

"Arthur, I never dreamed Jewel would be so frightened by your beautiful, black and white cat."

"It's a good thing I was holding Scratchy because I thought she would be frightened by Jewel. I never expected such spitting and hissing, and that was after she took one look at Jewel. It sounded blood curdling!"

We pledged to make new, unexpected plans to keep them separated for a while.

Whenever the two accidentally bumped into each other, it was always Jewel who fled in terror to find refuge on the upper level of the house. We were all anxious about each subsequent meeting the animals had until I spoke with my dear friend, Jane. Although not a licensed zoologist, she had plenty of experience raising cows, goats, horses, dogs and cats on her farm and her diagnosis and prognosis were reassuring.

"Jan, don't worry about a thing," she promised. "The two pets will soon acclimate to each other and they'll eventually be drinking out of each other's bowls. Give it some time."

We prepared for a long haul and were quite surprised at how quickly Scratchy stopped hissing, which made Jewel much more comfortable being around her. Before we realized it, they had trotted up to the boys' third floor enclave together, which turned out to be their favorite spot in the house.

Uniting two gaggles of kids into one new family in a new home became our next challenge after the pet problem was resolved. During school summer vacations and holidays, many conflicting relationship contests arose among the teenagers and twenty-year-olds.

"What are we failing to do?" I said one night to Arthur.

I was sobbing by then.

"Jan, take it easy and think about it. After all, we're blending two different family cultures into one environment. You're expecting too much, too soon.

"Your kids can't get over the fact that I'm not cooking the typical gourmet meals they are used to. My four sons never heard that word before—gourmet—let alone tasted really good food, especially during my law school years."

"I really feel sympathetic with Lynne," said Arthur, "who is really putting up with a lot of tricks as the only female among a team of sports fanatics."

"It sure is a lot of testosterone for her to deal with," I said.

"How do we divide all the jobs around the house?"

"What are the curfew rules?"

"What should be our new laundry priorities?"

"Who is driving which car?"

"How to enhance better harmony among the two tribes in this environment of two lovers and a house of strangers?"

These were just some of the questions and issues that were tossed around among all the inhabitants of 130 Fisher Road. Let's just say it was *complicated*.

Arthur and I found a solution that was right at our feet. A light bulb went off when we recognized that if a feline and a canine could gradually ease into a familiar life pattern and become compatible, without speaking each other's language, humans, could, too. We gathered all six of them at a family enclave and set out the ultimate house rules.

"Listen up," we both instructed, one at a time, "If Scratchy and Jewel can now drink from the same bowl, without asking permission, then there's hope for you, guys, too."

"Here's the new game plan," Arthur announced. "Don't even think of coming to either your mom or me with complaints about each other or help with resolving disagreements. We are no longer available to settle your problems."

"If a dog and cat can resolve their problems then so can you," I said, "because you speak the same language, remember?"

Arthur nodded.

"So, don't involve us, anymore," I said.

We were staunchly adamant about maintaining this new rule, based on our animals' changed behavior and its positive effects on everyone. Arthur and I stuck to our motto of non-involvement and disengaged from settling disputes. By stepping aside and letting democracy rule among our six children, now ages 15 to 22, we copied the brilliant example of our respective pets to great success.

Today, the original six, plus their spouses and fourteen children, are a united family of twenty-five because Scratchy and Jewel set our family standard twenty-eight years ago.

Ode to Be Sixty

While the magic number sixty sends shivers
Down the spines of the female populous,
I am welcoming, with joy, not quivers,
This big life event, feeling non-plus.

For I have earned each grey hair pushing through
My DNA dictated brunette crown.
I've finally reached the moment to be true
To no one else more important in town than ME!

After years of pleasing others
This magic birthday allows the luxury
To freely express to all, my "druthers"
Rather than, everyone else's priority.

I now speak my mind with new assurance
About what I feel, not what I should say.
Life's experience created confidence,
Reinforcing my sixtieth birthday.

REINVENTING MYSELF

I have earned the respect of many friends
By character displayed and standards set
When adversity happened to descend,
I searched for the silver lining, you bet!

It took sixty years to develop my skills
To be a better child, parent and wife,
Bubba and friend: trying to spread goodwill
And add positive energy to my life.

I've accomplished so much in many fields:
Teacher, nursery school founder and the law,
Which added wisdom to power, I did wield
As I faced down the challenges that I saw.

Added to all this mix, a board member's role:
Service to community, next in line,
When Aldersgate Youth Services did call,
I worked it into my schedule, in time.
Something's omitted from this "auto bio"
Tales of my hobbies, somehow neglected?
Of antiques, and dolls, I'm in the know,
Adding to collections well respected.

So here I am so proud of the sixty
Birthdays, that I've had to celebrate,
I face the future feeling as nifty
As I did when I was just fifty-eight!

My Elusive Claim to Historical Fame

I RECENTLY READ THE OBITUARY of Dr. Paul Brucker, former President of Jefferson University, who I first met while attending a lecture at the Union League. I was so excited to tap him on his shoulder to initiate a conversation and share an amazing discovery I had made a week earlier in San Antonio, Texas. I was convinced that my revelation would impact the history of Jefferson's medical school and add a feather in my cap for making the connection.

"Excuse me, Dr. Brucker, but I recently returned from visiting The Alamo and discovered that one of the heroes who died there was a graduate of Jefferson Medical School."

"What?" he said. "That news amazes me. I visited The Alamo recently during a medical convention and never noticed any such reference."

"Well, I even copied down the information from the glass showcase, displaying the effects of Dr. John Purdy Reynolds. The label said that he graduated from Jefferson Medical School."

"You seem too serious to be kidding," said Dr. Brucker. "I was right there and certainly missed it!"

The Alamo is a small church, which occupies a special place in the hearts of all Texans. The famous cry, "Remember the Alamo" commemorates the Texans' fight for independence from the Mexican government. The main room of the mission contains numerous waist-high, glass-topped tables, exhibiting the personal belongings of some of the slaughtered defenders.

The showcase of Dr. Reynolds included three medical textbooks, a stethoscope and his small satchel, containing medical supplies. Prominently displayed was an identification card with his name and information about the date he graduated from Jefferson Medical College in Philadelphia in 1828.

When I visited with Arthur, he teased me for stopping to copy down the information from the ID card on the showcase.

"Jan, don't you think they know all about this at Jefferson? It's only been over a hundred and sixty years after the battle! Come on, we've got a lot to explore and you're wasting time."

"Hon, we'll never know unless I write this down and find out."

A week later, I was trying to convince another incredulous man that Jefferson Medical School had a real connection to The Alamo. Dr. Brucker took a moment to regain his composure before responding.

"I'll be so delighted to put you in touch with our school historian, who will follow up on your report."

The very next day, I was contacted by Dr. Frederick B. Wagner, Jr., who was so excited to record my personal observations that he kept pressing me for more and more information.

"I'll contact you after I've connected with The Alamo officials," he promised. "This is the first we've ever heard that one of our graduates was one of the heroes there."

A few weeks later, I received a full report. What was fascinating, in addition to the fact that I had made a valuable discovery, was that Dr. Wagner had secured the attendance records of Dr. John Purdy Reynolds at their medical school, dating back to 1828.

"Get ready for a surprise, Mrs. Felgoise," he said. "Our records show that Reynolds never graduated from medical school. Back then, the curriculum was a two-year course and the second year was identical to the first. But guess what? Reynolds never returned for the second year, so he was never granted a medical degree."

"I'm speechless," I said.

"I shall have to inform The Daughters of The Alamo, the governing body of the historic site, that they will have to revise their information regarding this Alamo hero," he said.

The following month, my discovery and short-lived elusive claim to fame was predominately featured in *The Jefferson University Alumni* magazine. I was awarded accolades for my persistence in transmitting the information to the medical school, which resulted in the factual story about the "doctor" at The Alamo.

When I handed the magazine article to Arthur, he had a novel reply.

"I'm so glad that I insisted that you stand there and take those notes at The Alamo, all those years ago."

We shared a good laugh over that.

"I think I did more damage than I ever intended," I said. "Maybe I put history into perspective by correcting the misconception about The Alamo doctor, John Purdy Reynolds. Look how the discovery about his credentials, revealed because of me, created discomfort for everyone. Jefferson's claim that an Alamo hero was their famous graduate was dispelled; the Daughters of The Alamo had to revise their historical facts, based on Jefferson's report to them; and even the Reynolds family had to adjust to these new facts about their ancestor."

"What a trifecta," said Arthur.

"Yeah," I said, "my great historical discovery, which I had hoped would be my claim to fame, backfired in the worst way."

That marked the end of my unofficial career as a historical sleuth. Since that episode twenty years ago, I have shied away from pursuing any further historical inquiries. But it was yet another example of how Arthur and I enjoyed each other's adventures.

At Seventy

At seventy, I am more savvy and solvent but
Less sexy and serious than I was at sixty.

At seventy, I am more confident and composed but
Less circumspect and critical than I was at sixty.

At seventy, I am more literate and liberated but
Less loquacious and lackadaisical than I was at sixty.

At seventy, I am more altruistic and articulate but
Less apathetic and affected than I was at sixty.

Right now, I've reached my inner self,
Revealing the true essence
Of the whom I was meant to be, at seventy.

How I Worked My Way Through Retirement

IN 2008, WHEN WE REACHED the agreed upon golden age of seventy, Arthur and I retired from our respective positions, he from his accounting firm and me from my law office, we were all set to step out and see the world until his reaction to Parkinson's Disease brought us to our knees.

Due to the muscular inadequacy of his epiglottis, which failed to close off the passage of liquids and food to the lungs during swallowing, he developed continuous stream of infections. As a result, he underwent a series of eleven hospitalizations involving intubations in the ICU, which led to his death in 2010.

To maintain my equilibrium, I commenced courses at Montgomery County Community College and pursued my interest in a relatively new profession—Life Coaching, a field that had been blooming for about ten years. Many psychologists had already shifted to include this developing alternative into their repertoire when health insurance companies reduced payments for the psychological services included in their plans.

One day, my instructor advised our class.

"Don't just call yourself a Life Coach. Try to concentrate on a specialty feature of interest to distinguish yourself from others offering inspiration and guidance."

I sat and pondered his challenge.

What special background area can I use to assist those trying to resolve decisions and reduce stress?

Okay, keep going down that road.

Wait a minute; what have you been doing for more than twenty years? Your specialty has been divorce law. Now use it!

I jumped up with excitement to share my self-discovery with the class.

On that day, I began my path to becoming a divorce coach. My website was created by my teenaged grandson, Brett Felgoise. It featured a navy background with a white sailboat sailing serenely on a sea.

"Coaching Puts New Wind in Your Sails to Navigate the Seas of Divorce."

That was my central theme, printed in white letters. I was on my way!

I sent out introductory letters about my new retirement career to former legal associates, offering to assist their clients by alleviating the emotional stress related to the divorce process, which most lawyers neglected because of time restraints or a lack of interest.

What made me unique was that I conducted my coaching over the telephone, which reduced costs and eliminated trips to an office. Soon, I was dealing with out-of-state clients, relatives of those in Pennsylvania, as I worked with the personal complications of the divorce process, not their legalities, which these coaching clients also sought to relieve.

While initiating my new business, I was still working regularly as a mediator for Montgomery County Court, which had been an inspiration during my law career *and* through my retirement.

Of all the areas of Pennsylvania jurisprudence, only one area of law exists—custody—when a court may order mediation to help parents attempt to resolve their issues before resorting to litigation.

Pennsylvanians have no clue that directly across the Delaware River, the New Jersey courts order *every* entity, which files any complaint, to attend mediation before they are allowed to enter a court room!

This process involves both parents meeting with a court appointed mediator, without their attorneys, to try to resolve custody differences by working out a resolution that will effectively eliminate future court appearances.

Imagine yourself as a camera in the room when a mother and father first meet the court-appointed mediator in his or her office. Although sitting directly across from each other, they are oblivious to the other's presence and focus only on the mediator. That is, until, a magic moment occurs during the session.

Eventually, the parents casually face each other for direct communication and a real resolution has a chance to begin. I smile when this moment occurs, which it usually does, and routinely jot down just how long it took to occur.

After explaining the purpose and plan of the mediation, I ask if both parties desire to continue with our meeting, because mediation must be entered into voluntarily. My role at this point is to create a business meeting format of civility and discussion so an agreeable resolution may be achieved by both participants.

By this time in the process, I'm just an observer in the room, clarifying issues with my questions. The parties each take a turn to present their issues and if a topic isn't resolved they move on to the next one on their list.

Although every mediation doesn't end in a complete agreement, there are typically many examples of issues, which can be resolved, such as telephone contacts, vacation schedules or children's birthday celebrations. When the parties reach a partial or complete resolution of their custody issues, the three of us complete a Memo of Understanding, which the parents leave with, unsigned, to have their respective attorneys review. Parents also complete an Exit Survey, which evaluates the mediation, and is turned over to the court.

If you are the camera, you are now recording smiling faces as the parties depart, having successfully resolved all or some of their custody issues. But the last face to be filmed is mine, smiling from ear to ear, jubilant about another successful resolution. I waltz out of the office, feeling as if I am flying, fulfilled with the knowledge that another couple has learned some new skills to navigate their future custody agreements.

In addition to all of the legalities associated with my life, I also happily luxuriate in enjoying my grandchildren's accomplishments and activities. Grandparents do a great deal of boasting, but how many can beat my record? I am so fortunate to have thirteen grandchildren living within twelve miles of me, with just one far away in the Boston area.

Before high school graduations this year, there were four college students, four high school students, three middle school students, two in elementary school and one young man gainfully employed in Philadelphia.

As the Bubba of this squad, I really enjoy joining their parents at sports events to increase the volume and energy of their cheering squads, as we make ourselves known in the respective school district auditoriums or on their athletic fields. Birthdays, anniversaries and special holiday celebrations keep me running from one household to another, to pet family dogs and a cat and find out the new adventures of my brood.

How lucky I am!

Life After Arthur

MY JOURNEY TO MATURITY has been arduous, sobering and lonely.

Arthur's leadership was so integral to our lives, as he managed everything with such efficiency. I merely danced around, creating fluff, fun and plenty of enjoyment for both of us.

My great joy was watching him usher newcomers through our house as he led them "on tour," delighted to point out the paintings we had collected and the unique features we created. I always marveled at his "architecturally pure" sense of décor and the pride he displayed in our home and its eclectic frivolities.

Just a few months following Arthur's death, still in mourning, I did what felt impossible at the time by traveling alone to Florida to visit my Aunt Desna, who had been ill.

All I had to do was navigate the small West Palm Beach airport and stay with her in her condo. That turned out to be the "trial run" for my real flight into heroics, when I attended Jeff and Julie's wedding in March of 2011 in Chicago!

Navigating O'Hare International Airport was a greater challenge than my earlier trial run to Florida. I booked a hotel on Michigan Avenue, instead of the wedding party location, to enjoy the action of such a great city. I visited with Joe and Phyllis Reenan, Bruce Lincoln, my former Elkins Park Jr. High student, now a professor at the University of Chicago and was the second Bell of the Ball at the wedding.

The sadness of Arthur's absence at this long-awaited event was balanced by the joy everyone felt at Jeff's union with Julie.

Following the example of my coach, Phyllis Sissenwine, who rose up from her shiva for her daughter and immediately resumed her coaching career, I started back with my own coaching work after observing shiva for Arthur.

Phyllis inspired me to do grief therapy and assisted me with plans for coaching clients and developing new business, which I did after attending coaching meetings and developing my own prospects.

On my own, I discovered a pathway to assume the roles Arthur had always taken when it came to financial decisions about my future. I interviewed five sources for investment plans and secured an independent certified financial planner.

I planned a "Financial Freedom Workshop," led by Beth D'Andrea, and invited 10 women to attend. I decided to work with Beth as my financial consultant in lieu of the male representatives from conventional investment companies.

Attending the AIPAC Policy Conference in May 2011 in Washington, D.C. was a transformational weekend! I met Senator Joe Lieberman and his wife, Hadassah, long- time friends of Marc, and many other amazing people from all over the United States.

Upon returning home, I was recruited to attend a meeting at Beverly Cohen's home in Harleysville to give an analysis from an AIPAC "newbie" point of view, where I was applauded for my enthusiasm.

Soon after, I contacted hospital support groups to set up speaking dates. I even prepared newspaper PR releases for Penns Woods Retirement Center. Aviva Jaffe, Harriet Cove and I were engaged to appear at the West Chester Senior Center, Doylestown Hospital Support Group, AJ's Parkinson's Support Group and Harleysville PD Support Group, in addition to the Pennsylvania Hospital and a Veteran's Hospital panel discussion. Aviva and I attended the Pennsylvania Hospital PD Symposium and I attended two lectures by Teva Pharma, delivered by Dr. Daniel Kremens.

I also volunteered to assist at the Maccabi Games held in Philadelphia, where 1,200 Jewish teens from all over the U.S. and Israel participated in sporting events. Brett entered the swimming competition and hosted four boys at his home. I dished out lunch at the community center in Lower Merion.

I've added many new notches on my belt of independence and maturity, stemming from my new philosophy which unfolded after Arthur died:

"Complete the most difficult task of the day *first*."

It's the philosophy Arthur used throughout his life. I learned to tackle everything and tried to break my habit procrastinating. Even driving on Route 476 and the PA Turnpike became easier once I developed more confidence in myself.

Not bad for a widow in her 70s.

During the thirty-day mourning period following Arthur's passing, I attended Friday night services at Kol Ami and found comfort and solace in the music and chanting. I continued attending until the outdoor summer services began, which ended for me when the mosquitos decided to feast on me. That was the impetus for my decision to participate in attending B'nai Mitzvah class to learn how to do a Torah Reading, which I did two years later in March 2013.

Reaching out to long-lost friends became another notch on my growth chart. Eleanor Mastroll came first after I found her address while visiting Renie Burdetsky. I also wrote to Judy Novins Brown, who encouraged me to go to law school back in 1983. I last saw her when Arthur and I traveled to Minneapolis for Lynne's graduation. I tracked her down through her Florida phone and we had an instant hook up and joyous conversation! I also reunited with Joan Gordon, who Arthur and I had visited each summer for years.

Who can remember why we ever ceased our relationship? The best news is, we revived it!

I also committed to doing mediation for the Montgomery County Custody Court. I met clients at Brian's office in Jenkintown or Marc Gold's office in Bala

Cynwyd. I developed an easy plan to work with parents fighting over custody. I worked hard to convince them to refrain from going to court and to resolve their own issues. I also used Brian's office for private divorce mediation clients.

My greatest challenge was helping Glenn handle his divorce issues. At first, I bemoaned the timing of their family implosion, during Arthur's shiva week! I carried on about that until I realized that nurturing Glenn helped pull me out of my grief and pain so that he could move on with his life. I overcame the depths of my own despair, self-pity and grief and became a supportive mother, first and foremost.

Our relationship grew closer as our family closed ranks. The disappointment and shock of the divorce shifted my focus when my "Woe is Me" paralysis morphed into the loving action of a powerful woman.

On New Year's Eve, I chose to welcome 2011 with dear supportive friends and my brother and sister-in-law. We all sat at the dining room table and shared a slew of famous Arthur stories and how it felt to go forward without him.

That night, I was so proud of the new me and where I was heading on my new journey to maturity.

A New, New Year's Resolution

ARTHUR DID SO MUCH FOR ME during our life together and even after he passed.

One day, I was scrambling through the house, rushing to the front door from the kitchen, loaded down with two trash bags in my hands. I never made it to the front door. Instead, and quite dramatically, I must admit, I tripped on the edge of a throw rug in the foyer. The bags and I flew upward in perfect unison, flying like a helicopter until I landed on the rug, which was covering a stone floor.

There I was, covered in trash and bags, sprawled on my left side across the length of the rug, crying out like a quivering, wounded puppy.

"Oh, no!"

No none was around to hear me. I quickly took stock of my welfare—no snapping sounds from a possible break, and no pain along my shoulder and thigh, which had supported my body weight as I crashed.

"Arthur did it again!"

That's about all I could manage to say, but it was perfectly accurate. Once more, I had been saved from serious injury by my dear, late husband, who, even in his physical absence, had resumed his job of rescuing me from my "trips," those frequent moments when I tended to lose my balance.

A few years had passed since he had made a habit of rescuing me from the serious consequences of those careless falls. Once I began to concentrate on slowing down, thanks to him, and taking more time to travel from point A to point B, I hadn't experienced any more "faux pas while walking."

This latest incident wasn't a minor trip. I exhaled a sigh of relief when I realized I had fallen on the rug instead of directly on the stone floor. I hate to think about what my condition might have been if I hadn't been so lucky. Although I believed that Arthur's "intervention" had prevented any serious injury, I started to think about how I could have gotten help, if I needed it.

"Where is that safety contraption, Jan?" I asked myself.

Of course, the medical alert alarm pendant was neatly tucked away in the foyer desk drawer, far from my reach and still in its box. It certainly wasn't around my neck where it belonged, to be used in case of an emergency. This scary episode started me on a new road of safety precautions.

Taking immediate action after my emotional recovery, I put my new battle plan into action. First, I contacted my four sons to make sure they had the combo to unlock the safety lock box on the back door to gain access to my house. Then, I recovered the emergency necklace, issued by my alarm company, and secured it around my neck. All it requires is a touch of the button and the alarm company is signaled to call the police to come to my rescue. I resolved unconditionally to wear it every time I entered my home, without fail.

Once I regained my composure, I thought about how important it is to be prepared for the unexpected, especially when living alone.

The day had started out in jubilation because I spent it with family attending my oldest grandson's graduation from his master's program. I shivered, just thinking about how it could have ended!

Without my firm belief in my dear Arthur's "safety embrace from up above," I could have easily suffered a dire physical injury, leaving me without any assistance to get help.

"From now on," I said aloud (and to Arthur), "I'm protecting myself."

I wouldn't expose myself to this kind of needless risk any longer because it was time to ensure a better safety program. By adding a new "necklace" to my vast collection of jewelry, I had assured myself of securing help if ever needed it.

I've learned over and over again that it's never too late to make a new, New Year's Resolution, even if you make it in May.

My First Year, Sans Arthur

11.20.2010 – 11.20.2011

"Non compos mentis" means out of control.
I'm controlled, but my compass is not, yet.
Settings, directions and paths are tuned
to my re-configured tempo and order
as I tackle a new business approach
for managing my home and my life.

I never dreamed a new persona
could emerge from the tragedy of my loss.
Necessity demanded that I recharge,
and learn to manage our homestead
as I adjusted to family crises and loneliness
without the support of my loving bulwark.

Arthur plotted the marriage course
we traveled so smoothly together,
taking my hand and pointing the way.
While sensitive to my window dressing,
he was steadfast in his piloting role
to direct our "born again" nuptial cruise.

REINVENTING MYSELF

Shocked out of grief by emergencies,
I mimicked motions like Arthur would
and tackled the most difficult, first.
Developing my third career as a coach,
I strengthened loving ties to dear ones
and reveled in the kindness of friends.

The "new me" unfolded through solace
found in Shabbat services and Hebrew study,
As my body gratefully responded to exercise.
asking for help was new to my repertoire,
just like handling the many plaudits received
along my discovery route of this unique year.

Eat the Frog

Arthur Havsy's death has irretrievably changed my life.
No matter how ill he was, he was here for comforting,
his presence real, our partnership secure.
I have forever lost my lover, best friend and soulmate.
Inconsolable, I am. Shattered.
I face the last stage of my life alone and frightened.
Adjust, I must, and so I do,
with the newest theme of my life:
"Eat the Frog First."
(Tackle the hardest task first.)

This crisis requires a new conceptual approach.
I must be more self-reliant, independent and motivated,
I must continue to grow and welcome change.
I must face alternatives that I, alone, devise.
I must plan my life into my eighties.
And I shall, and I must.
And so I begin by eating the frog.

*Jan's Brushes
with History*

Part 4

Terrorism at the Twin Towers
September 11, 2001

JUST BEFORE 10 A.M., I headed to the lunchroom in my law office at the Bellevue in Philadelphia. One of the secretaries bumped into me as I opened the door from the corridor.

"A plane just crashed into one of the Twin Towers in Manhattan," she said.

"Oh, My God!"

I ran past her into the room, now crowded with people surrounding the TV set. Cries of horror bounced off the walls as we watched the black smoke encircle the impact point high up in the building. More and more people entered the room as the sounds of anguish flooded the space.

Before we knew it, the second building was hit in a giant explosion. The reality was quickly recognized, that this was not an accident! No one could function in the small crowded space surrounding the monitor and most of us left for our own computers for better access to the screen. We watched the ensuing nightmare of crumbling buildings, which cascaded to the ground, creating an enormous dust bowl.

None of us could have tolerated being alone amidst this tragedy.

I was still in my office with three associates when my phone rang.

"Mom, it's Brian. I want you to meet me at the parking lot of my building because we're leaving town immediately."

"Are you kidding me? My office isn't closing."

"Mom, I don't care, we're getting out of Center City right now."

Eventually, the Mayor of Philadelphia called for the evacuation of our city and with that formal announcement, I headed for my son's office. We waited in line for a couple of hours to claim his car and joined the endless procession, which exited the city, still not comprehending the experience we were living through.

When I collected my car at the Jenkintown train station, I headed directly for instant relief: my favorite antique shop in the neighborhood. I needed salvation and absolution from the nightmare I had been experiencing.

The minute I walked into the shop, the dish of keychains on top of the front counter caught my attention. As I fished through the small collection, one item stood out—a large, white plastic fob, attached to a key ring featuring the illustrious Twin Towers, soaring into the sky behind them.

On top of what I had just experienced, this shocking coincidence was too much. I paid for the key ring and ran out of the shop to head home.

We will all remember where we were on 9-11.

Virginia Earthquake Felt in Philadelphia August 23, 2011

AT TWO IN THE AFTERNOON, I was sitting at my desk in my home office at 151 Woodpecker Road in Jenkintown, wrapping up some business as it pertained to my new career as a divorce coach after my recent retirement from practicing family law. I had just completed my notes from a telephone conference with a client when I heard some strange clinking sounds, like glass hitting against glass. I swung around to see what was making that funny noise and saw objects on my computer desk, opposite where I sat, reverberating against the desk surface, which was situated along the outer wall of the house.

"What the heck is going on?"

The clattering sounds continued amidst the various collections, which were now reverberating against each other on the shelves surrounding the walls of the office.

"Is someone drilling outside in my backyard, without my permission?"

No reason to be alarmed. I later learned it was just a 5.9 reading on the Richter scale, announcing an earthquake! This surprise phenomena had rumbled its way north from Richmond, Virginia, and ultimately poked its head into Pennsylvania by sending shock waves to our town!

What a unique event, something we had never experienced and something I'll never forget. Fortunately, there was no serious damage to any of the buildings in our state. However, the multitude of small, porcelain, tin, crystal and china knick-knacks proudly and profusely displayed on shelves and tables throughout my home were the only objects which felt the shock waves.

Luckily, there were no abrupt movements of the house foundation and the only items which reacted to the quake repercussions were these numerous small antiques scattered throughout my house.

Miraculously, not one precious object d'art broke. Piled next to each other in great profusion, they ignored the total brunt of this unique spasm of nature, which travelled so far to make such a distinct, unique first-time impression.

REFLECTIONS

My "Slam/Dunk" Philosophy of Life

BECAUSE BOTH OF MY PARENTS were tall, I was predestined to find a place at the end of the line whenever we marched anywhere throughout our elementary school. In that position, closing ranks at the end, I had a unique opportunity to observe all the action in front of me. If there was too much congestion at one door, I would notice our teacher swerving our line to form a new path. From afar, I noted that if she saw a traffic jam at the nearest steps, she would move us to another exit.

Luckily, I was aware of all of these shifts in direction, as I looked out over the heads of my classmates. But I never dreamed how useful this experience of adjusting goals would be as I developed my personal "Slam/Dunk" philosophy in life.

Of course, this expression is normally related to basketball, as we picture the exquisite, smooth movement of the talented players who are able to "jam" the ball into the hoop. Kudos especially to the Philadelphia 76ers who have done that so well for so many years. I won't mention any names because God forbid, I should leave out one of your favorites.

I have adopted "Slam/Dunk" as my motto in life to reflect how I have survived and weathered a few of life's "Slams" with my retaliatory "'Dunks," which have inevitably led to success. I credit this rationale to my early opportunity to have witnessed, from the end of the line, as a young girl, the positive effects of changing direction and being flexible.

For example, I was seriously thrown off my game during college when my friend, Naomi announced with great joy that she been accepted into her desired sorority. When I told her with great disappointment that I had not been accepted, she flipped her attitude immediately and said that she would not accept the invitation she'd received. When I protested, she wouldn't hear it.

"Oh, Jan, no!" she said. "I won't accept for sure."

"Are you crazy!" I said. "Of course, you'll pledge; you've been tapped."

"Not without you, I won't."

We argued for hours and then days and Naomi refused to relent. If I wasn't good enough for that sorority, then it wasn't good enough for her. Such was my luck with friends. Because of this "Slam," I found another outlet to release my energetic skills and perform my "Dunk."

I became involved in The Women's Student Government Board at college and worked my way up to the Vice-Presidency of the organization. I was even delegated to represent my school at a collegiate conference and was flown to Chicago in my senior year.

Bert Felgoise and I married during spring break of my senior year at Penn. Upon graduation, I was fortunate to have snagged a prize-teaching position at Elkins Park Jr. High, which I attributed to the relationship Bert still maintained with his old principal, who hired me. Long ago, in a distant age, female teachers who were married usually worked for two years and then retired to start their families. Not us.

Bert held me close.

"Look, Hon, I know how you might feel about starting a family, but right now, until I finish law school, you're our famous bread winner. Then I need a couple of years to get on my feet before we can financially think about getting pregnant."

"Honey, I'm on the same page as you. Your plan is my plan and I love my job and have no problem waiting until we can afford it."

I faced the reality of our "Slam" situation with renewed energy and pursued a master's degree. I even earned Merit Teacher status in the district and was appointed department head in my sixth year of teaching.

What a "Dunk!"

Just when things were going well, according to our planned unique schedule, I suffered a major "Slam" in the form of a miscarriage.

Almost five years later, I approached Bert one day with an observation.

"Can you believe this new blond baby boy is ours? It's so hard to believe that if I didn't have a miscarriage years ago, we wouldn't have ended up with these amazing four boys."

My teammate and I had scored another "Dunk." Actually, four of them, and one more was all we'd need to have our own team in the NBA.

Our family's greatest "Slam" occurred when Bert died suddenly at home from a heart attack at age forty-six. In addition to the shocking tragedy, I had to contend with closing his law practice and settling with a bank over an outstanding multi-million-dollar mortgage for a housing project he was promoting.

The banker stared kindly at me.

"Mrs. Felgoise," he said, "we don't intend to foreclose on your home right now as it was the guarantee for the outstanding construction loan. At present, no builder has come forward to underwrite the deal and assume that mortgage. They all expressed interest in purchasing the housing project, one lot at a time."

"Even our best friends, the Stompers Builders?"

"Afraid so. They'll go for the project, but only one parcel at a time."

Our house was ultimately saved, and we squeaked through our financial crisis by learning a key lesson: Friend or not; in business, you don't pay retail when you can purchase at a fire sale.

My awesome "Dunk" from this dire experience was my "Jan of Arc" decision to protect my family of four sons by going to law school. I had no idea how this plan would manifest itself and be fulfilled, but at the time it was my solution for resolving my situation.

"Jan, be serious," said most of my friends, "who is going to hire you as a forty-five-year-old, freshly minted attorney by the time you graduate?"

A scant few, led by Naomi, sang a different tune.

"It's a great idea, Jan!"

"Thank you," I said. "I'm already enrolled."

With a firm conviction to "Dunk" my way through Temple Law School, I began what became a successful legal career, based on my experience learning to shift gears and embrace change, which I had gleaned from all I witnessed as a girl from the end of a school line.

Marrying Arthur and joining our two families together became a supreme "Dunk." Somehow, we were able to achieve our goals through fun and games, with laughter and tears aplenty until my latest "Slam" when Arthur passed away.

Someday, I may finish another book, called, "Two Lovers and a House of Strangers."

Stay tuned for my next "Dunk."

A Father's Day Tribute

To Edward Edwin Goleman (1907-1979)

LET ME RECORD SOME SWEET MEMORIES of you, Dad, here on Father's Day 2019, as a loving tribute to you on this special day.

Your smile was always infectious and the ever-ready twinkle in your eye filled me with constant joy each time I detected it aimed in my direction. I loved being the apple of your eye, despite a few shortcomings in my youthful behavior. Although I don't recall the exact details of one incident in particular, I can recount why this indiscretion is so memorable.

There we were, one sunny summer day, relaxing in a rolling-chair on the Atlantic City boardwalk. I was almost three years old and my face was protected from the sun with a new blue bonnet that matched my fluffy dress. I balanced myself on your lap. You were seated next to your dear friend, Uncle Sol. Of course, I called all your friends and Mommy's "Aunt" and "Uncle" as was the protocol long ago for children.

After about two hours watching people stroll by in our rolling-chair, which was secured against the boardwalk railing, I had an accident. I knew right away that I had done something I wasn't supposed to, as I felt my pee-pee seep through the layers of my pants, slip and dress, right onto your lap.

There was only one thing I could do, and boy did I cry! Of course, you knew right away about my accident. Then the strangest thing happened. As you held my dripping body in the air, Uncle Sol saw your wet lap and started roaring with laughter. You eventually joined in and even my mournful sobs quickly turned into giggles. You carried me home, holding me horizontally under your arm so your shirt sleeves wouldn't get wet from carrying me under my legs.

I can never forget how graceful and safe you always made me feel.

Summers in Atlantic City provided many fun-filled memories of you as I matured. People-watching was a popular sport for parents, especially on Saturday nights.

Mom would get all decked out in her mink-stole, wrapped around her shoulders, and you were suited up, too, lounging in your reserved rolling-chair, lined up with hundreds of others against the boardwalk railing.

I was about ten years old and so happy to stand in front of your feet, greeting friends of yours who strolled by amidst the crowd.

The best part of those nights was walking home at almost ten o'clock from the "boards." Hand in hand between you and Mom, we almost danced those few blocks while belting out songs together. Sometimes, which seemed like always, you and I got carried away and began yelling out songs while sashaying along the avenues toward home.

"Eddie," Mom would hiss, "tone it down, you're too loud. People are staring at us."

"Let 'em stare," you'd say. "We're having a ball singing our songs."

My yelping giggles at this remark just encouraged you to sing louder—to my glee and Mom's consternation.

It seemed to me that you played the better of two roles as a parent. You had no need to be a disciplinarian because all you had to do was say something quietly, once, and I would jump. Mom wasn't as fortunate because the older I became the more I tested her rules.

For some reason, I never ever questioned your decisions. There was something about the definitive way you declared a rule that meant business. Besides, you didn't spend as much time as Mom did, dealing with the antics of a gal growing into her teenage years.

I especially enjoyed our morning drives to my high school. After we dropped Mom off at her elementary school to begin her day teaching, I would jump into the front seat and become your co-pilot, sitting close beside you as we took on the events of the world in our discussions. Once I began driving, you would slide over as soon as Mom departed, allowing me to take over the driver's side and assume control of the steering wheel.

This tradition extended for an additional three and a half years while I commuted to the University of Pennsylvania in your car. That opportunity to be alone together solidified our dynamic-duo relationship to perfection. How fortunate I was to have this special time to question your family history and learn how you worked with your siblings to help with their desperately needed financial support.

The most fascinating tale you told was how you used your fists to maintain your claim to the special corner in your neighborhood, which you felt you owned. It was from this busy intersection that you sold daily newspapers at six in the morning, before attending classes at Central High School.

"Move on, you dirty Jew," your adversary would shout at you. "I want this corner for my paper sales."

"Not without a fight," became your frequent mantra, as you charged ahead at those brutes. Those numerous episodes of fighting actually paid off, as you were so proud to relate. You became interested in boxing and entered many amateur contests as a young adult.

All those bouts reached a crescendo thirty years later when our family traveled to Penn State University to watch Joel compete in the ring as a heavyweight boxer representing his college. There was not a prouder father in the audience than you, Dad. You always claimed that your son inherited your boxing DNA.

Your hobbies were also fascinating to a young girl like me. Although I never accompanied you to the golf course, where you pursued your favorite sport with friends, one member of our family did have that experience. Our dog, Cookie, accompanied you and Uncle Sol every Wednesday morning for a round of nine holes at Cobbs Creek Public Golf Course. By the time I arrived home from school, Cookie had already collapsed into her two-day siesta, overwhelmed with fatigue.

Remember Dad, you walked only once around the course's front end, but Cookie had to respond to your whistles by running back to you and then taking off again. She raced four times around to your one time golfing those holes, until exhaustion set in and you had to practically carry her home.

My golf course experience included fun-filled memories of joining you every Sunday at Green Valley Country Club. Mom would drive Joel and me in the late afternoon to meet you for a family dinner at our golf haven. We explored all the unique rooms featuring gambling machines, and a "one-armed bandit," and we even peeked in on the card players so absorbed in their heated games of gin rummy, before playing the pin-ball machines and romping around outside, playing miniature golf.

I especially remember the pride you exhibited when you gave me away at my wedding to Bert. You applauded my efforts to continue teaching so he could attend law school after his military service.

But nothing matched your joy of adding our four sons to Joel's two daughters, giving you a grand total of six in your menagerie of grandchildren. You loved roaming around with the boys in our large backyard, hunting for praying-mantises, pitching balls during baseball practice and swimming in our pool, teaching tricks to your little dolphins.

Sadly, in your late sixties, you fell under a dark net of illness and were forced to submit to all forms of medical treatment. It was comforting for all of us that Joel took on the task of helping to steer you through your treatment by delving into research and planning doctors' conferences and new treatment trials.

I always thought that my last visit to you in Florida, during your final hospitalization, was well planned. I awoke one morning from a dream that you were in trouble. Shortly thereafter, we received a doctor's call. Mom and I rushed to the hospital just in time to say farewell. When we arrived, you had already succumbed to a ruptured artery, induced by former X-ray treatments to your neck.

Although I was filled with grief, I desperately hoped that you recognized the two loving women who were with you and felt their love by your side.

Dad, I will never forget all the educational moments, joyful celebrations and your unending, uncompromising love. Keep watching over us all!

My Valentines

SEVERAL YEARS AGO, after reading a sensitive and charming Valentine's Day article by Nancy Davidoff Keeton in *The New York Times*, which she used to thank the important men in her personal history, I became inspired to recall how the boys and men in my life helped me to become the woman I am today.

Edward E. Goleman (Goldman)
What a daddy I had, wrapped around my finger! Yet your power was so great, you never had to raise your voice, as once was enough, whatever it was. Thanks for teaching me how real men treated their wives because that set a standard to be emulated. You were my hero!

Joel Bernard Goleman
Brother, I reveled in calling you "Butzie," your camp nickname, which caused you great consternation. I never thanked you much as we were growing up because my teasing always ended up with punches, yours on me. Once, you even stuck me with your lead pencil and we had to run to the doctor to prevent blood poisoning.

I was so proud of your operating skills when you mesmerized the neighbors with surgical experiments.

By the time I was in high school and could really interact with you, you were off to college, the Air Force and marriage, which limited our relationship. Only later, when we were both parents and married, was I able to work some wonders and influence you.

Any time there was a family crisis, we were there for each other and I appreciated that comfort. You took over Dad's medical care and decision making as he battled cancer. I think you made as many decisions as his doctor about the treatment mode conducted.

I'll never forget the riot under the chuppah that you created at my wedding to Arthur after walking me down the aisle, when you nudged my four jokesters who nearly lost control of the whole thing. By some miracle, the ceremony got under way and we were legally married.

I often laugh when as a mature man you changed your moniker to "Joe" from Joel, something to analyze, one day. Thank you for taking my advice when needed, and when no one else could get you to change, and for helping me when I asked for it, too.

Herman Goldman

Uncle Hank, you were the task master who teased me all the time because you really didn't know how to handle little girls, especially as they kept getting older.

I remember seeing you in a captain's uniform when you came home after World War II to Grandmom's apartment on 59th and Carpenter Street.

Thank you for your generosity to match my Board of Education scholarship to UPenn. However, I always felt so awkward because I had to call you each semester to remind you to send your check in time for registration.

At that time, Dad worked for your plastering company, McGleister & Goldman, which created some family disharmony for Mom, who thought you should compensate Dad better than you did.

He never let that bother him because you were his favorite brother who could do no wrong. Actually, you were both reliving an early business relationship as Goldman & Goleman, which was why Dad changed the spelling of his name in the first place. However, it's my understanding you were equal business partners.

You always got a big kick out of being around the boys when we visited you down at the shore. You enjoyed calling out numbers 1 through 4, in place of their names, which you never got straight.

Far from being warm and fuzzy, you were a presence to be dealt with. Your smile was your biggest asset, especially with the family, and you commanded our respect because of your business success and luxurious lifestyle.

How Fridays Changed My Life

MY FRIDAYS BEGIN like every weekday. My plan for the day is forged the night before when I prepare for work as a Montgomery County Court mediator to help parents resolve their custody disputes. In addition, I might have pre-arranged telephone conferences with clients to work as a divorce coach, the business I created when I retired from my law practice. What is so comfortable about my retirement career is that it is based on my pre-planned time schedule. It leaves me plenty of opportunities to visit my thirteen local grandchildren, meet for excursions with friends and participate in many study group activities.

But my Friday evenings are restricted to one specially defined scheduled activity and this practice led to something extraordinary for me some years ago.

"Hey, everyone, heads up for a special announcement I have to make."

I delivered this command at the large Thanksgiving table in 2012, with the entire family all around it paying attention.

"I've been attending a B'Nai Mitzvah class at our synagogue, so in less than two years I shall become a Bat Mitzvah!"

"Bubba, you're supposed to be 13 to become a Bat Mitzvah," said Samantha, who was preparing for her own special day. "Aren't you a little too old?"

"Well, when I was thirteen, girls weren't permitted to read from the Torah in our synagogue, so here's my "golden" opportunity!" I said. "Besides, I want to experience the same Mitzvah all my grandkids have either had or are preparing to go through. Now, I'll be able to help everybody with the Hebrew portions."

That announcement shocked my family into learning about their 70s Bubba who was pursuing the same religious ceremony as they did when they reached that magic age.

All 25 members of my immediate family, plus other relatives and friends, gathered at the synagogue to cheer for me when I celebrated my B'at Mitzvah in 2014. I beamed with pride, as I took turns with my ten classmates, chanting from the Torah, on our special day. Although it was unusual to delve into this Jewish ceremony at my age, I soon took another leap into Judaism that changed my Friday evenings to this day!

I would have been the last person to imagine that I would attend Friday evening services, every Erev Shabbat, at my synagogue, Congregation Kol Ami! Just what instigated this commitment? Was there some mystical magnet that initially attracted me to attend weekly services?

No. I attribute my new, strictly structured Friday night activity to my sheer joy of the peacefulness I feel from the calming elements of the prayers. My new immersion into this Jewish ritual of attending services happened so quickly after my B'at Mitzvah that it felt like I was pulled into Judaism by an undertow.

The soft strumming of the guitar strings, rendered by our Cantorial soloist, Rebecca Schwartz, sets the tone by enveloping attendees with ancient melodies even before the service commences. You can feel the religious unity of togetherness permeating our small chapel as everyone rolls out Hebrew words to the beat of the stringed instrument.

Because of what I learned for my B'at Mitzvah, I'm now able to follow the Hebrew and participating gives me great pleasure. I sway with the rhythm of the music and utilize my soprano voice to belt out melodic tunes with new assurance.

There are also quiet times, when the arc is opened, exposing the Torah as we offer prayers of thankfulness. That's when I experience novel emotions. This new calm has a magical affect as it wraps me in the pride of my Jewishness.

Sometimes, during the service, my mind wanders from the pages of the prayer book pages and I get caught up thinking about departed loved ones, to whom I silently talk. What a wonderful feeling to feel all of this in a sanctuary!

In addition to my emotional development and the evolution of Judaism in my life, attendance at Friday evening services is also intellectually stimulating. Rabbi Eliot Holin always introduces historical information or spiritual topics for discussion. He also encourages us to deviate from the service when we discover a passage in the liturgy that appeals to our curiosity.

"You can always catch up with the current prayers."

What a refreshing invitation!

Since I have become something of a family expert in Hebrew, I receive quite a few telephone calls for help from my grandchildren. Haley's questions stimulated me to write this piece as part of my memoir class.

"Bubba, can you review the 'Shehechiyahnu' prayer, with me? I can't figure out how to say some words in the last two lines."

"Sure, hold on until I grab my prayer book."

My dream has come true—to help my grandchildren—which was the exact thing I intended by becoming a Bat Mitzvah. I am also experiencing the unexpected personal bonus of a new peacefulness and joy, which I have discovered in my bond with Judaism.

The Road to Eighty

It's hard to believe how many roads I've traveled
From birth to this wonderful celebratory day,
My fun-filled life will begin a journey to unravel
In this presentation, my life's adventurous replay.

I was Eddie and Esther's little girl, Joel's younger sister,
Who lived a life of luxury on Carpenter Street.
When my Nanny left, I was so blue and missed her
Until I skipped third grade and again became upbeat.

Bryant Elementary School was my proving ground
As best friends and great marks set the stage
For class-officer jobs that followed me around
In West Philly High. winning every elected wage(r).

Great scholastic goals helped me win the surprise:
Senior Grade Director was my top-class role,
Scholarship to U of P was my favorite prize,
Voted "Most Likely to Succeed" just rocked my soul.

JANET GOLEMAN FELGOISE

Off to Penn which I completed in three and a half years
Just in time to marry Bert, man of my dreams,
Graduated with "Hey Day" award to everyone's cheers
After honeymooning amidst Nevele Resort's, streams.

Elkins Park Jr. High began my teaching career
Because Bert took me to meet his old principal.
I even became department head during my six years
While he set up his practice, after Temple Law.

I had the best reason to retire and stop work
As a baby boy, Marc, appeared on the scene.
Motherhood wasn't a challenge which I did shirk
As months later, we welcomed, Roy, our second dream.

A brand-new home, with pool. in Albidale, H.V.
Plus, my job writing for "The Breeze Newspaper"
When in less than 2 years, Brian joined our family
Until, Glenn made it four boys just a little later.

It was a great time to add another boy to our group,
So, Aunt Rose and I brought home, our Spaniel, Rex,
This guy enriched our lives with joy and spook
As he always ran out the door, seeking puppy sex!

I started Childtowne Montessori with four friends,
Formed Brandeis Book Club and became
V.P. of the Library Board, next.
President of Art Goes to School; will activities ever end?
Not until CISV which made our teenaged boys perplexed!

REINVENTING MYSELF

Three Temple Judea Bar Mitzvahs
and splashy affairs were celebrated
Until our family tragedy and we suddenly
lost our dear leader, Dad,
Glenn's manhood ceremony was rather understated
As we tried hard to recover from our bereavement,
so sad.

I became a substitute teacher at Lower Moreland High.
Although others may have suffered, I had a ball,
Despite the real fact that Marc and Roy deeply sighed
To find their Mom teach their classes and walk their halls.

"Jan of Arc" found a solution to resolve our legal morass
Of selling Pine Woods and closing Dad's law practice, too,
I'd go to Law School to solve all problems fast
As this new career would provide solutions and clues.

Years later, from out of the blue,
guess who should appear?
Why, my old third-grade lover, Arthur,
who was a widower,
Who came courting me and soon made it perfectly clear
That our lives would be enriched if we were together!

A gorgeous Tudor home in Jenkintown was in store
For our big new group: six kids, plus Scratchy and Jewel,
Lynne and Jeff joined the Felgoise famous four
As eight of us created a set of new blended-family rules.

Soon our children's weddings just added to our mix
Of welcoming new family members and their groups,
Grandchildren came spewing forth and added tricks
Learning to say, "Bubba" and "Zeydah" without spoofs!

Becoming a lawyer was a thrilling, satisfying new role,
Working with three bosses in my twenty-plus year career,
Filled me with rich experiences to brag and extoll
My professional life, helping free my clients from fear.

My retirement in '08 was a prep for our years to travel,
But dear Arthur's passing played havoc with these plans.
So, I created "Divorce Coaching" to ease my life's pall
And became a Bat Mitzvah,
so religious study could expand.

Finally, here I am at eighty, a Mediator in Custody Court
Although only part-time, this job keeps me hopping.
As I also offer 11 kids, my emotional support
And plan to "Bubba" 14 grandkids without stopping!

Parting Ways

THERE ARE TWO WAYS WE LOSE loved ones: either through hearing about their death or by being close enough to actually watch them pass away.

One day, when I was five years old, neighbors came to visit my mother. They sat in our living room on the many extra chairs squeezed between the furniture, quietly talking. I didn't know why so many people were coming in and out, but I heard them in the next room as I carried on with my dolls.

Then Aunt Reba came into the room.

"Janet, please don't be so loud. Your mother is feeling very sad because Grandpop died."

Although I had learned about "died" when I lost goldfish with names and when my brother "lost" two chickens we kept in the basement, I didn't make the connection about people.

Back then, we didn't have Mr. Rogers on TV to share the death experience with children and our parents certainly didn't. When I had seen my mother crying days before, she told me that Grandpop had "passed away" but her enigmatic message to spare me had gone right over my head. After Aunt Reba's comment, I was still clueless about the connection between "passed away" and "died," so I kept playing with my dolls and curbed my noisy dialogue.

Fifteen years later, when my grandmother died, I was well-aware of the downward spiral of her health and expected her impeding demise. I spent time with her in her bedroom as her health failed and participated in her funeral and shiva. By then I was deemed old enough to be involved in handling family loss.

When my father was hospitalized while vacationing in Florida, I was initially reluctant to leave my four sons, aged seven through twelve, to fly south to be there to assist my mother.

Fortunately, I was able to be present to comfort her and help handle the complicated funeral arrangements to transport Dad back to Philadelphia. I was grateful, in fact, as taking care of these details helped me overcome my immediate sense of mourning and loss.

It didn't take long for the loss to catch up with me.

In my early forties, our family's beloved father and husband, Bertram Melven Felgoise, passed away after suffering a massive heart attack in the middle of the night. My screams woke all four of our sons, who ran into our bedroom to witness their worst nightmare. Their father died at the hospital while medical aid was being administered. The boys, all teenagers, and I made all funeral decisions together and the five of us selected his gravesite. We were overwhelmed by the outpouring of community support from our neighbors in Albidale, along with family, friends and schoolmates, who helped us handle our loss at the funeral in our synagogue, Temple Judea, where more than five hundred people were in attendance.

By the time my mother, Esther Litvin Goleman, died, at age 91, I was monitoring her care at home. She had been failing after recuperating from a broken hip and was finally placed in hospice care in her condo. My brother and I supervised her health-care companion as we lived nearby and were constant visitors.

One day, after receiving a phone call about her precarious physical condition from her aide, we rushed over to be with her. By that time, the visiting nurse was there, and we were advised that she was resting comfortably.

"Why not use this opportunity while you're together to explore final arrangements for her, when you're not under pressure? She's resting now with stable numbers and nothing's going to happen."

We looked at each other, thought the nurse's recommendation was viable and set out to visit a funeral home before we fell into the clutches of chaos. The showroom was filled with numerous coffins, lined up, arranged by price, from one end of the room to the other. We were quoted numbers for each selection we pointed out and as we became more comfortable in this bizarre environment we loosened up and started joking!

"Do you really think this box is worth a thousand more than that one?"

"I'm more impressed with the darker color wood than the lighter color."

"Can you believe we're carrying on like this?"

As we whispered to each other, we felt more and hilarity, until we spotted a shiny, silver-colored coffin at the end of the room.

"You're not going to believe this one" I said, "It's metal."

"It looks like a huge silver catering container to warm food," Joel said.

At that moment, all we could do was laugh when we learned how many thousands of dollars "that one" cost. We both felt like actors in a surreal Woody Allen movie, as we finished touring the funeral home and made our selection. This was a scene I've never forgotten.

When we returned to my mother's condo after this bizarre shopping spree, we were still "high" and feeling okay with everything, until we heard the astonishing news that our mother had died while we were gone.

"But she was sleeping so normally when we left," I said. "How could she?"

"She slipped away peacefully," the nurse said.

After the downturn of parting with these dear, family loved ones, my life lightened up when I married Arthur Harold Havsy at age 50. About twenty years into our wonderful marriage, Arthur's health became compromised by Parkinson's Disease, which had gone undiagnosed for years, when it began to affect his swallowing. This created frequent lung infections, requiring numerous hospitalizations in intensive care.

On the morning of November 22, 2010, I awoke to find that Arthur had passed away during the night. I cried out to his nurse, sleeping in the next room, who rushed into our bedroom to comfort me.

A five-year reprieve from suffering the loss of a loved one ended when my brother, Joel Bernard Goleman, succumbed unexpectedly to sepsis, a wholly unexpected blood poisoning from an infection in his elbow.

What made his death so surprising was his amazing medical background. He used this knowledge so expertly in all decision making related to our father and his wife's medical handlers. Because he always monitored his potential health problems by dosing himself with unique vitamin treatments, we were caught by surprise when he suddenly died in a hospital emergency room.

His death was just the beginning of more losses in his immediate family during the next three years.

Joel and Barbara Wekselman Goleman's younger daughter, Caren Goleman Strong, died in November 2017 from cancer, which had been discovered during surgery in March of that year. She fought valiantly against the spreading encroachment of this disease and after receiving chemotherapy in her New York state hometown, she expired peacefully at home with her husband, Eric Strong.

At that time, Barbara, my sister-in-law, had been residing with her daughter, Myla, and son-in-law, Chris, who rescued her from a badly run assisted-living facility. She had recuperated and was walking again, but she deteriorated rapidly after suffering a stroke while contending with pulmonary issues. Barbara passed away in February 2018.

Out of necessity, from losing so many significant people, I have built up a reservoir of strength and emotional resilience to handle parting ways with my loved ones.

The Epitome of My Legal Career

MANY ACHIEVEMENTS COME TO MIND when I consider my twenty-five-year career as a family lawyer. I was fortunate to work with three legends in our area, and despite the dire predictions I heard about my job possibilities upon graduating from law school in my mid-forties, I found instant and highly gratifying employment, first with Fred Cohen, then with Lynne Gold-Bikin, and finally with Neil Hurowitz—three men I consider Olympians of domestic relations law.

Among many special moments I had during my years of contributing to these practices, one highlight supersedes them all, and had nothing to do with either one of my great teachers. My proudest career accomplishment relates to my favorite client, Rudina, and the task we accomplished together.

About twenty-five years ago, Rudina, her husband and their young son were fortunate enough to win a lottery ticket to emigrate from Romania to the United States. Rudina and I met one summer when she entered my life as a replacement for my housekeeper, who had referred her. Rudina had been working as a substitute teacher in Philadelphia during the school year, as she had been an educator before coming here.

I suggested that she investigate the Computer School for Adults, as I had heard it was a great starting place to begin a new career. Soon, she enrolled and began her studies with great enthusiasm and success, eventually graduating with honors. Her first job required an arduous, two-hour carpool commute each way to a location near Atlantic City. After perfecting her performance there, she moved to another job in Philadelphia, where she kept advancing.

As her marital problems developed and intensified, Rudina and her son, Albi, separated from her husband and sought my legal advice. That's when the story of my greatest accomplishment of my legal career began, aided by my loyal, young friend.

Because I was not a partner at my new firm at the time, I could not bring Rudina in as a pro bono client in order to provide complimentary legal service. Obviously, she couldn't afford to hire a lawyer while saddled with the burden of child-care expenses for her son. I solved that problem by engaging with her in what I referred to as "extra-curricular" legal education classes.

To prepare for her support action, which she was forced to initiate because the father of her child wasn't paying any child *or* spousal support, we resorted to telephone tutorials after each working day, which continued for many weeks.

The first order of business was to refute the father's claims of financial inability to pay support because his construction business was failing. At my suggestion, Rudina became an unofficial private investigator. She took pictures of the father's new truck and car, which she could present at the support hearing. We role-played, with me portraying the judge and practiced questioning the father about his business success, as evidenced by his "aforementioned" new truck and car. Rudina's courage and resourcefulness provided all the inspiration I needed during our lengthy and numerous phone calls.

The father's pleas of poverty to escape his support responsibilities were represented in court by the aspiring, incoming chairman of the Philadelphia Family Law Section of the Bar Association. Once they were finished, it was Rudina's turn to face this primed, very experienced opposition—alone. As she relayed it to me, she took one step at a time to present all of her questions, which would produce the proof we had prepared to dispute the father's claims. Her carefully plotted evidentiary case exposed he opponent's fallacious testimony and was only topped by the judge's question to the father.

"Sir, what is in your back pocket?"

"My cell phone," he mumbled.

With that, justice was served! The judge banged her gavel loudly on her desk before announcing her decision.

"You are hereby found to be falsifying the economic condition of your construction business, founded on the evidence presented by the Plaintiff. Therefore, your support obligation will be based on the support guidelines of both parties, and you are hereby ordered to pay arrears based on that amount since the date of separation."

That evening, Rudina and I screamed for at least an hour on the phone, as we celebrated her legal accomplishments in court! Just before we hung up, full of joys from her victory, Rudina shared the opposing counsel's comment to her, which he offered in a state of disbelief after the proceedings had been finalized and everyone was leaving the courtroom.

"Who helped you prepare for this hearing?" he said.

Without skipping a beat, Rudina gave her reply.

"I learned it all on the Internet!"

My protégé certainly outperformed me with that response, which I would never have thought of like that right there on the spot!

After twenty-two years of family law practice, I retired to my own new business of divorce coaching. I continued my part-time work for Montgomery County Court as a Child Custody Mediator whose passion for mediation can sometimes be infectious!

The Unexpected Courage
to Reinvent Myself

I DON'T MEAN TO BRAG, but I *am* proud of my accomplishments and if you don't mind, I'd like to review some of them here and point out that my road to independence has been paved by many others. When I think back on my development as a child and how it led me to who I am today, I must begin with what I learned through solving problems in second grade. First, I had to face the music of my mother's wrath when she discovered I had been "shoplifting" erasers from my teacher's desk. The initiative I took to remedy that situation and ease my mother's anguish taught me quite a valuable lesson. I escaped the mortification of my teacher detecting my crime and paid a debt for my wrongdoing through the shame of disappointing my mother.

My next burst of growth was connected to my entrepreneurship in selling lemonade at a roadside stand. I borrowed our family's brand-new, silver ice bucket and promptly (and quite accidentally) punctured it with the ice pick I was using to chop the ice. I suffered the pain of making a quick profit and losing it all and ended my money-making project after pledging to purchase my parents a new ice bucket.

In elementary school, I began my political career determined to be friendly with my classmates so I could parlay my popularity into winning activism. I was elected to various class offices and became a teacher's favorite in many classes, most notably with Miss Rome and Mrs. Cantor. I worked my way up to the office of treasurer of Sayre Jr. High and my first important speech was at our graduation. I was sorely disappointed when my father arrived late and missed most of it because he was attending a political meeting in Philadelphia.

My real growth began at age $14\frac{1}{2}$ when I journeyed by myself on a train to a summer camp in Asheville, North Carolina. Mom's fellow teacher, Jules Goodison, smuggled me into Camp Osceola under the pretense that I was sixteen. I was on my own, not as a camper as I had been at age 11, but as a junior counselor dealing with counselors who were working on graduate degrees while teaching school. That Christmas, I traveled again by myself to Miami to visit my new (mature) gang of friends and stayed with Eleanor Maitlin Mastroff.

I continued my dramatic career moves at West Philadelphia High School where I was elected grade director in eleventh and twelfth grade. I was voted by classmates as "Most Likely to Succeed," received the Gift of Roses for service to the school, The History Prize, and a Board of Education Scholarship when I graduated in 1956. On top of all of these accolades, Uncle Hank

Goldman matched my scholarship to the University of Pennsylvania.

At Penn, I immersed myself in women's student government, tried out for *The Daily Pennsylvanian* newspaper, participated in our School of Education activities and was "bitten" by Bert Felgoise, not necessarily in that order. I represented our department as president of the honorary education sorority, Kappa Delta Epsilon, at a national convention in Chicago.

I earned my first real paycheck working at Zavelles' Book Store for two weeks each semester during the book purchase rush as new classes formed. That whopping check represented my first earnings other than some infrequent babysitting jobs for 25 cents an hour. I took advanced courses in the summer and graduated in three and a half years in June 1959 after winning The Women's Hey Day Award Ceremony Education Award and having my picture published in *The Philadelphia Inquirer* marching down the aisle with the prize.

After marrying Bert in 1959, I began teaching and became the family breadwinner as Bert attended Temple University Law School. I developed real leadership skills at Elkins Park Junior High by becoming a merit teacher and acting English Department head. It helped that I had the inside tract to become the favorite teacher of my principal, Dr. Herman Wessel, because Bert had been a famous Jr. High student at the same school.

Motherhood created another new area of leadership as there were only two other women living nearby who could boast about a gaggle of four sons. In the late 60's,

I was invited to write a weekly article for *The Breeze*, a local Huntingdon Valley newspaper, which was intended to highlight the activities of new families in the area. I dubbed my weekly deadline pressure-cooker, "In the Valley," which I continued writing for many years.

Some people gain notoriety as "finishers," but I was a "starter" as I expanded my horizons even while raising my riotous family of boys.

First, I started a Brandeis Reading Group in my Huntingdon Valley neighborhood and then I channeled all of my energy to starting Childtowne Montessori Nursery School because there wasn't a Montessori school in our vicinity, and I wanted our sons to have that advantage. I invited ORT friends Linda Stock, Ilene Stern, Renee Gordon and Barbara Platt to form the Board of Directors.

Once the school was structured and we divided the workload of supervision, supply maintenance, financial responsibility, enrollment and teacher recruitment, our management tasks were easily divided into one-day-a-week responsibilities. I served as the President of the Board from its inception in 1969 until 1983, when I resigned to enter law school.

The next notch on my belt was starting the Lower Moreland Chapter of "Art Goes to School," which included studies at the Philadelphia Art Museum and planning meetings to prepare volunteers for teaching about the reproductions we introduced to students in our district. I participated in monthly meetings with other chapter heads and assumed responsibilities in the larger organization by becoming Chair of the Delaware Valley combine of 27 Chapters.

In 1976, I led a group of 22 of our members on a trip to London for a week-long art tour with Barbara Bernstein—*without* our husbands.

In 1980, I was invited to join the board of directors of the Huntingdon Valley Library. I later became its vice-president and publicized the library with what we called a Merchant's Week Campaign, which encouraged businesses to support our fundraising. After that popular, campaign, I answered an advertisement for a job with Boefinger & Associates, a public relations/marketing firm in Cheltenham.

I had every intention of wowing them with my superlative enthusiasm and "know how" and planned to talk my way into part-time employment, even though the position was full-time.

For my first assignment, I was supposed accompany Charlie Boefinger, the CEO, to a meeting of the Hershey Chocolate Board in Hershey.

I never made it that day or got to negotiate for a part-time position because I was felled by a mysterious fever from an alleged earache. My emergency surgery ended up revealing that my fever was due to an infected IUD and my hospitalization and recuperation abruptly ended my nascent advertising career. As it turned out, I met Mr. Boefinger twenty years later, when he became a client at my law firm.

In 1981, Bert had an attack of colitis just before we were to embark on our second annual Utah family ski trip. I took a deep breath and the five of us sallied forth on spring break without Dad. The boys took care of the skis and luggage while I handled driving to and from the ski lifts *without* a GPS. We survived a dead car battery at the mountain top, and I was proud of navigating our team, both on and off the slopes. Little did I realize how that experience would prepare us all for life without our team leader the following year!

When Marc was in high school, we became members of Children's International Summer Village (CISV), following the lead of our friends, Phil and Elaine Cohen. Marc joined an exchange group to Finland one summer and went to Japan the following year. Roy went to Sweden and Brian went to Finland. Poor Glenn missed out, as his trip to Costa Rico was cancelled due to political unrest. When Bert passed away, I became vice president of the Philadelphia Chapter of CISV and president the following year.

All of these learning curves played a role in how I survived Bert's sudden death in 1982. Somehow, I managed to handle an entire new set of challenges, from closing up the Pine Woods Construction Company to tackling the legal vicissitudes of selling the property, lot by lot, until Colonial Mortgage took back the land in a foreclosure, to working with Elaine, Bert's secretary, to close the Felgoise Law Office.

A year later, I jumped into my "Jan of Arc" role when I enrolled in law school, determined to become an attorney and forever "protect the family." I commenced my studies at Temple University Law School through the endorsement of Margery Broderick, the Assistant Dean and wife of the former Lieutenant Governor of Pennsylvania. Bert's political life and connections were a boon that forged that connection for me. Returning to school after an absence of 17 years was daunting, but I pulled it off and graduated with aplomb.

Life was delirious in 1988. My lover, Arthur Harold Havsy, had become my husband and we had started a beautiful life together with our blended family. I started a new job with Fred Cohen, Esq., in Center City. When he moved on to Blank Rome, I joined Lynne Z. Gold-Bikin, Esq., in Norristown. Three years later, I interviewed with Neil Hurowitz, Esq. He and I hit it off so well that I didn't go home after my interview but worked through the remainder of the day.

I'll never forget navigating a snowstorm in January 1993, and making it home from Valley Forge as possibly the only driver braving it on the turnpike. What luck it was two months later when Neil joined Astor Weiss Kaplan & Mandel, LLC and moved his practice to their Bala Cynwyd office. That shortened my commute by half, and I loved the proximity to antiquing every Friday at Pennywise Thrift Store in Ardmore. When we moved to their Center City office at the Bellevue Hotel in 1995, this began a new train commute and upscale shopping.

I enjoyed a short stint as a talent agent around 2000, while working at The Bellevue. Walking through the concourse from the train to the bus on the way to my office, I always contributed to the coin collection bottle situated in front of three blind singers and their seeing-eye dog who serenaded commuters every morning with fabulous renditions of harmonious tunes. They became familiar with my voice as I said "good morning" each time I passed, and we enjoyed several pleasant exchanges.

One day I asked if they would be interested in a "gig" for my office Christmas party, which they enthusiastically accepted. I contacted the Bellevue Management Office to talk about my "find" and the response they elicited at our holiday celebration. I figured, what could be a better Christmas gift to the patrons of the food court than the holiday renditions of this singing group? I sold the management on my idea and struck a solid deal to make sure they were paid well. Roy contributed new dress shirts, which added to the singers' holiday appeal. For one week between Christmas and New Year's, they provided a songfest, which lit up the food court.

I started the Lassies in 2002 as a private group to continue the fun of the Jewish Federation course I attended, called "Dealing with Life in Your 60's." Our original group of 10 women met monthly to discuss life challenges and we rotated hostesses who planned each topic of discussion. We met for many years and shared our joy, pain and love.

Over the years, I gradually reduced my schedule assisting Neil Hurowitz to three days a week, and at age 70, I decided to retire so that Arthur and I could travel. Parting from Neil's legal relationship after almost 15 years was difficult and I am forever grateful for the latitude in our partnership and the respect he awarded me within the fiefdom of his practice.

A luncheon date in 2005 with Merle Holman and Bobby Stern led me to initiate a group called Passionate Ladies. We focused on helping each other find a passionate match for the next stage of our lives.

Although I retired at the end of 2008, after twenty-four years practicing law, I maintained my license to continue working for Montgomery County Court as a custody mediator. Parents filing custody petitions are ordered to meet with a mediator before proceeding to a court hearing in an attempt to resolve their case before going to court. I developed my mediation practice for more than 10 years since taking the initial forty-hour training. I have always been passionate about how helpful the process can be for participants who value it as an alternative to litigation.

The next year, I formed The PD Dames to promote interest in Parkinson's Disease caregivers. Aviva Shigon Jaffee, Harriet Cove and I met for breakfast so we could inject some much-needed laughter into our lives, as each of us were caring for our impaired husbands. These raucous breakfasts allowed us to exchange ideas and lots of laughs, as we tried to solve several problems common to all of us. Our "Eureka" moment came when we realized we had some answers to share with other caregivers.

Voila! The "PD Dames Lowdown for Parkinson's Disease Caregivers" pamphlet was born. We reviewed, refined, and revised it for months, making sure we covered all areas of life and dreams related to caring for a loved one impaired with this disease. We refined our presentation before performing for the Pennsylvania Hospital Neurological and Movement Disorders Department's social service team of supervisors. They were knocked out by the concept and encouraged us to share our program with caregiver groups. Our show went on the road for groups like Bryn Mawr Hospital Parkinson's caregivers, Pennsylvania Hospital and Veterans' Hospital Parkinson's caregivers.

That same year, I investigated opportunities in Life Coaching by taking courses at Montgomery County Community College, where the instructors rekindled my interest in this field. I'll never forget the day I developed my coaching niche when an instructor urged us to select a specific area of expertise to distinguish our individual practice.

"What expertise did I have to develop?"

A light bulb exploded, and Divorce Life Coaching was born right there in class! The pursuit of this career became a sacred sanctuary for me during the 20 months I spent dealing with Arthur's illness. I learned to compartmentalize his medical trials while running on my own with the excitement of developing marketing plans for coaching with my own coach, Phyllis Sissenwine, who guided and directed my work.

In the summer of 2011, I received a call from an acquaintance who I'd known for years. I'd always commended the positive manner in which he and his ex-wife had dissolved their marriage by thinking only of their two daughters. My admonition to him had always been, "Peter, you have to write a book about your story," I told him.

"Jan, we *are* writing a book; Cairn and I are serious. And we want you to write the chapter about mediation."

I was thrilled and stunned. A new challenge was about to begin, another in a long road of independent ventures. As I bundle them together here, I can take some historical perspective to feel proud of my resolve and courage. After writing about these experiences and examples of creativity and dare-do-it-all, I feel like a new woman with a positive, exhilarative burst of enthusiasm about my future. I feel so fortified, bolstered, and encouraged about my ability to continue to work and set new goals for my life and the challenges that lie ahead.

*Jan's Brushes
with History*

Part 5

How I Relate to Covid-19

THE ENTIRE WORLD'S POPULATION of almost six billion people first fell prey to the ominous black cloud of the coronavirus pandemic, which began in Wuhan, China, at the end of December 2019.

During the same time period, after consultation with a physician and a subsequent CT Scan, I was advised that I had the pernicious pancreatic cancer, which had invaded my liver. It was as if the world sympathized with my medical affliction, or so I wanted to imagine.

Within a matter of months, each and every country in the world took measures to shut down, close off and isolate their citizen population in an attempt to halt the revenges of this fast spreading disease that recognized no national boundary.

Life changed for everyone: workers in every occupation and trade, parents working from home and children continued educational pursuits by being home-schooled or following school curriculums on-line. Professional practices closed and service centers operated solely online. Everyone made life adjustments, except essential workers on the front lines handling cases in hospitals to treat Covid-19 victims

At this very same time, I felt wild and free and beyond these prior restraints, as it was "essential" for me to drive three times a week for an alternative medicine protocol, investigated by my friend, Gerald Lemole, a retired heart surgeon.

I felt free, driving on the Route 309 expressway, smelling the newly minted flowers, experiencing freshly formed buds blooming on trees and observing empty parking lots. As I drove directly to the doctor's office and home again, I continually enjoyed the wide-open spaces without any traffic.

I shall always remember how lucky I was not to suffer from the effects of the initial shut down regarding the virus and my ability to navigate and feel free!

There's a famous saying that people look to in times of stress: "Misery loves company."

I felt instant relief, knowing that people all over the globe were suffering from all kinds of acute changes to their lives and I took comfort in the fact that I wasn't the only one with new conditions to contend with on a regular basis. I had plenty of company to commiserate with throughout the world!

ACKNOWLEDGMENTS

FINALLY, I, TOO, HAVE JOINED the throng of memoirists who have appeared during the past fifteen years and flooded the book market. However, not being a famous person, my principle aim is to provide my journey here in print so that it can be shared in the future with my grandchildren's grandchildren so that they can gather familial information, which their parents and grandparents might not remember.

As a new teacher of English and History at Cheltenham Township's Elkins Park Junior High, I had a great deal to learn about English composition, as I prided myself on being a history buff.

I give much credit to all of the Cheltemham Township adult school courses in creative writing and poetry, which infused me with new vistas of writing skills.

After four-and-a-half years of memoir writing classes at Keneseth Israel Synagogue's twice a week program, I was overwhelmed by how many episodes I had amassed from my family's numerous adventures.

"That's it," I exclaimed. "I'll create a book!"

"Are you kidding? How can you meld this collection into a book?"

Then I became connected to my famous book editor, David Tabatsky, from New York, who offered invaluable information about transforming an episodic journey into a smooth, connected life story.

Thanks to all of my fourteen grandchildren, who call me Bubba, and their moms and dads, who provided the inspiration for my desire to proceed with creating a cohesive life story.

Loving kisses to Brett Felgoise, Samantha Felgoise, Josh Felgoise, Bethany Felgoise, Brooke Felgoise, Brianna Felgoise, Benjamin Felgoise, Haley Felgoise, Lizzy Felgoise, Shane Felgoise, Jordan Unikel, Chase Felgoise, Nathan Unikel and Alyssa Havsy.

Parting Poems

I've always loved writing poetry,
and since this is my book, after all,
and I may not have another good chance to share these,
I'd like to leave you with five parting poems,
which speak to things near and dear to my heart.

Manic in Marrakech

It's hard to defend your senses from attack
By the shrieks and vivid hues, back to back
Which assail you with good natured intent
Blocking your views and refusing to relent
On confusing, deluding and sabotaging
A tourist's attempts to take it all in.

As sensual distractions create such a din
You can't figure out what to protect first,
When your eyes, nose and ears begin to hurt,
From the unique ranting flooding the atmosphere
Of salesmen displaying their wares, so dear
As you weave in a follow-the-leader-line
Through the Medina and Souks, one at a time.

You've taken this position as protection
From being separated, 'cuz without direction
You're lost forever in a myriad maze
Amidst narrow tunnels of seamless alley ways
Enticed by Arab silver and jewels which are displayed
But you dare not stop or you'll get lost by the delay!

Suddenly, you're flat against a carpet doorway
As a motor bike or car forces you to stay
At attention, until it speeds right away
Leaving you more breathless than before
From this shopping experience, you've tried to explore.

Finally, free, you're out in the Market Square
Breathing in real sunlight and jasmine air.
Thinking you're free of furious sounds
But wait, there's new excitement when you turn around!

Here, Whirling Dervishes twirl to loud beats
Of drummers revving up the performers' feats,
Snake charmers' pipes shrill through the mobs
As the serpents hiss out to cause loud sobs
From huge crowds gathered around in bright hues
Causing straining tourists to be more confused
About how to escape this riotous, loud clamor
While all their senses feel so very hammered!

So, they slink away to awaiting vans
Exhausted from all these sensory demands
Happy for some shut-eyed time to unwind
From this most challenging tour they will ever find!

Eating Humble Pie at the Barnes

Last year I scoffed at Barnes' arrangements
Of clustered master works of famous art.
Just too dumbfounded to make connections
Or figure out the essence of his plan.

But what a difference a year can make!
The DeMazia course opened my eyes.
With the know-how from "Informed Perception"
I've unlocked the secret scheme he devised.

First, he selected similar colors
As redundant themes throughout the pairing
Of paintings, linked by light, line and space
To decorate the phalanx formation on walls.

The pewter hinges encircling all
Mimic the sameness of shapes in paintings
That nestle together, tied by the core
Of similarity common to each.

Coming Soon:
A Premium on Death

When Steve Sanders, an insurance adjuster,
arrives at Grant House to evaluate fire damage, he
falls over the edge of the warped carpet. Threat-
ening to sue Gi-Gi for negligence, she allows him
to recover in the comforts of her home. While
healing from his injuries he meets a fate worse
than a sprained ankle. Someone hates the man
enough to murder him.

Although mayhem is the standard for life at
Grant House, a tribute game of poker, an eating
disorder, and four widows (past, present, and
future) raise it to the next level. There's no short-
age of suspects, including Gi-Gi. The death of
the insurance adjuster relieves her of the potential
lawsuit, but puts her in the position of having the
most to gain.

JANET GOLEMAN FELGOISE

Furniture pieces placed against the wall
Highlight colors and lines tucked away
In the surrounding pictures, all arranged
To fit themes he sought to capture.

I now pride myself with "cracking the code"
Of the Barnes Museum painting placement.
Plus, my new vocabulary now conveys
Just what the artist creates with pigments!

Dogs I've Loved
(and a Cat)

Cookie was my first.
Her only litter of puppies taught me about responsibility.
Besides the loving, there was work.
Clean up, clean up, and more clean up!
When I was 12, I painted an oil portrait of Cookie.
It remains among my cherished mementos.

As my youngest son graduated into big boy pants,
we found Rex, the most affectionate dog!
I figured, with four boys under reasonable control,
a dog should be no problem.
But I had never met the likes of
"Rex of Kensington."

After years of "never say die" persistence,
Rex finally stopped jumping up to kiss your cheek.
But he never stopped running away from home.
Rex Alarm!!!
Time for a fire drill in our neighborhood!

JANET GOLEMAN FELGOISE

Head down, tail stub even lower,
Rex slinked back home, banished to the laundry room.
Rex brought a sense of community to Albidale.
When the Rex Alarm bell clanged, he was everyone's dog!

Rex died in 1985, after suffering a stroke.
We brought him home and buried him in our back yard.
A clandestine affair, as it was contrary to Township rules.
"Please excuse the lateness of Brian and Glenn.
They had to attend the funeral service for a relative."

A year later, we found Jewel.
She was a "57" Heinz variety mongrel,
Her quiet, soft nature won our hearts.
When the Felgoise and Havsy families joined forces,
Jewel and Scratchy eventually learn to accept each other,

When Scratchy died, Jewel was left to fend for herself.
She soon became queen of the household.
That run last until she passed in 2002.

I've been so lucky to "mother" these wonderful pets.

Year Without Arthur #2

Can one steer a ship without a rudder,
or pilot a plane without a compass,
or walk a mile without a path?
I've done it all in this year without Arthur!

I had to think outside the realm of Jan
to mimic Arthur's moves and manage my life
as if he were still at the helm
smoothly steering the waters that lay ahead.

"What would he do?" became the theme
of the song I sang to overcome what I faced
and tried to tackle tasks with his mindset
as my new persona slowly emerged.

Oh, I'm so proud of how I've matured
by adopting his take on life:
"Tackle the hardest chore, first,
then the remainder will be easy."

JANET GOLEMAN FELGOISE

My mind relaxed in religious repose,
my body was rejuvenated with exercise,
as I relished the kindness of friends
and strengthened my ties to loved ones.

All the while adding notches to my belt
of new success, strength and growth
in my journey as a sole survivor
as I grew my leadership role in life.

I Lost Another Brother

The new cellphone voicemail, I didn't hear
As muffled vibrations obscured clarity,
Reporting the death of someone held dear
Creating panic and real cause for anxiety.

My attempts at "replay" to discern which name
Proved futile and just increased new fears,
It had to do with Kligermans, but "who" wasn't plain
Though I repeated the message, nothing was clear.

The recent loss of doggie, "Big boy" first came to mind,
Maybe that's what the caller tried to pass along?
Quaking, I kept pounding away, hoping to find
Whom I lost, then the relay; it was Ron who was gone!

My mind just refused to accept and compute
As we just spoke this past week, "It couldn't be!"
The news filtered through, though, I tried to refute
The truth of his loss which became my new reality.

The joyful voice of his, never again to be heard---
The playful repartee, each of us grateful to touch base
And share our mutual high school antics, so absurd,
As we exchanged trips and history, not to be erased.

We yapped about values,
character and all that life taught,
Like two philosophers, just smoking our pipes,
As we debated all issues of current political thought
Until we reached agreements, that each was right.

The pain of my loss is very heavy to bear
Until I think about his Nancy's challenges, unaided,
She must step right into the SCS leadership chair
To continue fulfilling the goals which they had created.

REST IN PEACE MY DEAR FRIEND/BROTHER.

Salute to Queen Esther

How do you do justice to a "living legend" in her time?
You start by heaping praise for the courage she displayed
When faced with adversity of the physical kind,
As she garnered strength
to meet the task to heal, unafraid.

Next, you repeat her tales,
which became a part of our family lore,
So that all the grandkids' children can someday replay
All the funny stories about Esther, whom we all adore
Which typify her personality, right up until today.

Then, you give thanks for how hard
she would always worry
And express concern for all of our escapades,
As we, kids and "grands" pursued life in a frantic scurry
While she found time to "qvell" with accolades.

Further, you relate the funky numbers
that emit from her pen
In contrast to the intellectual books
she boasts of having read,
And hope the reading talents are inherited

by her grandchildren
And not her numeral facilities,
for which we'd dread.

Also, you relay the admonition, "Esther, don't cry,"
Whenever moments of happiness
trigger her tears to flow,
Thus, causing all the family to laugh and sigh
As they offer handkerchiefs, into which she can blow.

After all has been said, you can count your lucky stars,
That you're related to or befriended by this octogenarian
Who's leading the pack by setting examples by far
In excess of what an ordinary mortal can "carry on."

We love YOU!

An Old Granny's Mammogram Fun

Dedicated to Nicole
at Mary T. Sachs Breast Care Center/Abington Hospital.
Thanks for making this experience so enjoyable.

Only Woody Allen would have the guts and gumption
And film a real-life event as memorable as this-
Of an old Granny's mammogram, for special fun
To guarantee an audience's absolute hysterics!

An 80-year-old's body parts have long adjusted
To the ravages of gravity and its slow pull,
Reducing her "titckas" (that's enough said)
To lack the strength to stand up and be full.

But no, this lady's "titties" must lift and rotate
As they fit the X-Ray Machine's tilting shelves,
For her body twists every which way, but straight
And ensures that the images do come out well.

Once the left view is filmed: shift again-
Just start anew with her chest's other side,

As body parts are pulled way up to her chin-
She's in for her second, unwelcomed, wild ride!

All this time, all she's doing is telling jokes
About this unspoken, wicked, torture chamber,
As it helps endure her body's stretches and pokes
By keeping her brain detached and slightly saner.

Released from the clutches of the awful Machine
She staggers slowly, with smiles, to the dressing room,
To don her clothing and start revving up to dream
Of hopeful good results, which can't come too soon!

Learning How to Talk to God

How to talk to God when you have no clue?
So, I think of dear Eric for inspiration,
Whose evangelic fervor is way overdue,
When he begins every conversation,
As he tries to inspire us to heaven's door.
But his talk to God's son doesn't assist
Other earthlings like me who need more,

So, I keep reaching up to beyond and persist.
While "I'm spiritual," moves me along
To offer prayers and be more involved
Along my path of singing ritual songs.
It's the music that calms my resolve,
Ending my week with peace and rest.
I'm vigilant trying to search for way more

So, I can reach up to touch my Jewish quest,
Endeavoring to learn how to open my door.
Our prayers are so very simple to recite
Enveloped by others' voices as we read
Aloud the written words which delight

As we all cry out our passions' need.
It's so easy to become swept along
By rote recitation from our books of prayer
Trying to reach the heights where we belong,
But while on my own, I'm just not there . . .
Yet!

33079043R00176

Made in the USA
Columbia, SC
07 November 2018